ARTIFICIAL INTELLIGENCE

COLLECTION

FROM IT PROFESSIONAL TO AI EXPERT

THE ULTIMATE GUIDE TO A SUCCESSFUL CAREER TRANSITION

Prof. Marcão - Marcus Vinícius Pinto

Disclaimer:

Please note that the information contained in this document is for educational and entertainment purposes only. Every effort has been made to provide complete, accurate, up-to-date, and reliable information. No warranty of any kind is express or implied.

By reading this text, the reader agrees that under no circumstances are the authors liable for any losses, direct or indirect, incurred as a result of the use of the information contained in this book, including, but not limited to, errors, omissions, or inaccuracies.

ISBN: 9798344597409

Publishing imprint: Independently published

Summary

Foreword

In recent years, artificial intelligence has ceased to be a distant technological promise and has established itself as one of the driving forces of digital transformation, shaping the future of industries and professions.

For IT professionals, this transformation brings unique challenges and opportunities. The volume you're about to explore, "From IT Professional to AI Expert: The Ultimate Guide to a Successful Career Transition," is an essential tool for anyone who wants to navigate this transition successfully.

This book is aimed at IT professionals who want to expand their horizons and reposition themselves in the artificial intelligence market. Programmers, data analysts, system administrators, and even IT project managers will find here a clear path to explore this new field, learning the necessary skills and identifying opportunities for growth.

It is not just a technical transition, but a true professional evolution.

Throughout the book, we address the reasons why AI is not just a trend, but a revolution. Professionals who understand how to adapt to this scenario will be ahead in the era of automation and intelligent systems.

The content begins with an introduction to the need for this migration to AI and how traditional IT functions such as data entry and technical support are being replaced by autonomous and intelligent solutions.

In addition to exploring the differences and similarities between IT and AI, the book also offers an ideal learning path, detailing the skills you'll need to acquire.

From fundamentals in mathematics and advanced statistics to mastery of machine learning, deep learning, and natural language processing (NLP), this guide is a practical source for understanding the principles that drive AI and how to apply them in real-world situations.

This volume is more than a technical manual — it delves into the challenges you may face along the way, such as the fear of failing in a new field or the mental burnout caused by intensive AI learning.

Among the most valuable aspects of this book, we also highlight the importance of building an AI portfolio, which is essential to make your skills stand out in the market.

With practical examples and clear guidance on how to create impactful projects, you'll be prepared to demonstrate your value in any interview or job opportunity.

This book is intended for:

- Programmers who want to migrate to the development of AI solutions.

- System administrators interested in automating processes and exploring autonomous databases.

- IT project managers looking to get up to speed on strategies based on artificial intelligence.

- Data analysts who want to move into machine learning and predictive analytics.

By purchasing this book, you'll not only be learning about AI, but preparing to lead and excel in an ever-expanding field.

However, this is just one step in an essential journey in the field of artificial intelligence. This volume is part of a larger collection, "Artificial Intelligence: The Power of Data," which explores, in depth, different aspects of AI and data science.

The other volumes address equally crucial topics, such as the integration of AI systems, predictive analytics, and the use of advanced algorithms for decision-making.

By purchasing and reading the other books in the collection, you will have a holistic and deep view that will allow you not only to optimize data governance, but also to enhance the impact of artificial intelligence on your operations.

Get ready to embark on a transformative journey and start working your way to becoming an AI expert.

Happy reading!

Good learning!

Prof. Marcão - Marcus Vinícius Pinto

Digital influencer specializing in soft skills for professional fulfillment of entrepreneurs, entrepreneurs, leaders and managers. Founder, CEO, teacher and pedagogical advisor at MVP Consult.

1 From coding to cognitive thinking: how artificial intelligence is redefining the role of the IT professional.

We live in an era where artificial intelligence (AI) is transforming from a mere automation tool to a disruptive force capable of redesigning entire economies, labor markets, and even the very structure of society.

What was once a field reserved for academic experts, is now being integrated into almost every sector of the global economy.

But what makes AI so revolutionary? And, more importantly, why is this technology becoming a natural and desirable transition for IT professionals?

Artificial intelligence promises more than process optimization. It is inserting itself into the heart of decision-making.

Unlike traditional IT solutions, which require explicit programming to solve problems, AI systems are based on algorithms that "learn" from data.

This means that IT professionals, who already have a deep understanding of data structures, operating systems, and networks, are perfectly positioned for this transition.

The AI revolution is not only technological, it is also philosophical: it requires a change in mindset, moving from the linear logic of code to the probabilistic and adaptive thinking of artificial intelligence.

In recent years, we have seen remarkable examples of this revolution.

Companies like Google, Microsoft, and Amazon are investing massively in AI by using it to create virtual assistants, optimize supply chains, predict consumption patterns, and even create art through deep learning algorithms.

This integration is transforming entire industries, and IT professionals who choose to specialize in AI are at the forefront of this transformation.

1.1   Why should IT professionals move to AI?

The transition of IT professionals to AI is not merely a career change — it is a natural evolution. The IT professional already deals with information systems, data management, and process automation; However, in the current paradigm, these systems require explicit rules and are relatively rigid.

AI, on the other hand, offers flexibility and adaptability through models that learn from data and continuously adjust.

Let's take the example of Amazon, which, in its inception, relied heavily on IT professionals to manage its digital infrastructure.

With the company's growth and the need for global scale, Amazon has adopted AI solutions to predict demand, manage inventory, and even adjust prices in real-time based on consumer behavior.

IT professionals who were part of this evolution needed to not only fine-tune their technical skills, but also understand how machine learning algorithms could replace traditional methods of process optimization.

A recent LinkedIn survey, titled "2020 Emerging Jobs Report," showed that the AI and machine learning engineer position is among the fastest in terms of global growth.

The report highlights that the number of AI-related jobs has grown by 74% annually over the past four years. This scenario offers an extraordinary opportunity for IT professionals who want to migrate to areas of greater complexity and strategic impact.

The decision to migrate to AI brings with it a series of advantages that go beyond the increase in salary or professional status. It represents a transition to a field that is shaping the future of humanity.

IT professionals who make this change not only increase their career opportunities, but also gain the ability to influence the world in meaningful ways, whether it's developing life-saving health technologies or creating solutions to global environmental problems.

1.2   Beyond automation: the end of careers or the professional renaissance in the age of artificial intelligence?

The arrival of artificial intelligence (AI) is promoting a profound transformation in the labor market, especially in sectors related to information technology (IT).

Beyond the simplifying discourse that alludes only to job replacement, it is crucial to reflect on the impact of AI with a critical and analytical lens.

1.2.1 The role of autonomous systems and the erosion of technical support functions.

In recent years, level 1 technical support – the one that covers more basic tasks, such as simple problem-solving and initial guidance to users – has proven particularly vulnerable to the advancement of AI technologies.

Chatbots and virtual assistants, powered by natural language processing (NLP) algorithms, have been taking on an increasing volume of these activities.

Apple's Siri and Amazon's Alexa are examples of widespread systems that represent this evolution. These technologies can solve common technical problems without the need for human intervention, freeing up IT teams to focus on more complex tasks.

A study conducted by consulting firm McKinsey & Company predicts that in nearly a decade, most companies will have integrated chatbots capable of performing up to 80 percent of Tier 1 help desk interactions, with a degree of efficiency and accuracy superior to that of their human predecessors.

IT professionals who currently work in these roles will have to reposition themselves, learning to manage and customize these platforms, acquiring skills in dialogue design and conversational AI systems.

1.2.2 The rise of automation: OCR and the extinction of data entry.

Data entry, once a crucial and time-consuming task, has become one of the first functions to feel the effects of automation.

With the development of optical character recognition (OCR) systems and NLP, the digitization and interpretation of textual data, previously done manually, now occurs automatically.

Companies like ABBYY and Google are at the forefront of this revolution, using these technologies to process millions of documents in fractions of seconds, eliminating the need for human operators.

The impact is clear: within 3 to 7 years, it is highly likely that most data entry-focused positions will be defunct or substantially reduced.

However, deep analysis of the situation reveals that with automation comes new opportunities for professionals who decide to expand their skills in areas such as data science and predictive analytics.

The key here is the transition from a purely technical role to a strategic role, where knowledge about AI tools is combined with a critical and creative view of data management.

1.2.3   Software testers: from manual operations to automated testing.

Traditionally, software testers played a crucial role in identifying bugs and performance issues before a product was released.

However, automated testing tools, powered by machine learning algorithms, are quickly taking over.

Tools like Selenium and TestComplete already use AI to create test scenarios, perform repeated tests, and even predict potential failures based on code patterns.

This automation reduces the time required for manual testing while increasing the reliability of the results.

The future of these professionals will depend on their ability to reskill.

Those who learn how to integrate automated testing tools into their workflows, adjusting and customizing the algorithms for specific scenarios, will be better prepared for the future.

The idea is not just to replace manual labor, but to redefine the human role as supervisor and optimizer of AI systems.

1.2.4   Database Administrators: The Era of Autonomous Databases.

Database administrators (DBAs) are about to face significant disruption with the introduction of autonomous databases, such as Oracle Autonomous Database, that promise to manage and optimize themselves without the need for human intervention.

Routine tasks such as patching, performance optimization, and backups are now being automated, minimizing the demand for routine DBAs.

However, as in other areas, AI does not eliminate the need for human intervention, but changes its focus.

DBAs who specialize in the areas of security and optimization of autonomous banks, or who acquire skills in Big Data, will be better able to navigate this new scenario.

Data security in an AI-driven world will become an issue of critical importance, and those who can provide insights into how to protect autonomous banks will play a vital strategic role in organizations.

1.2.5   Repetitive Task Schedulers: The End of Manual Coding?

With the increasing adoption of low-code and no-code development tools such as Microsoft Power Apps and OutSystems, coding repetitive tasks is becoming obsolete.

Generative AI also enters this field, with tools like GitHub Copilot, which is already being used to automatically write and complete code based on minimal human input.

Simple tasks like scripting or tweaking repetitive functions are being impressively automated.

For programmers who previously focused on mechanical tasks, the future looks challenging. However, the ability to collaborate with AI tools and direct them to solve more complex problems will be a key skill.

Professionals who focus on systems design, software architecture, or integrating AI into technology products will be able to remain competitive in a market that values innovation more than manual execution.

1.2.6   IT Project Managers: The Transformation of Planning with AI.

Lastly, traditional IT project managers are also being impacted. AI-enhanced tools like Asana and Trello are taking over many administrative tasks previously performed by these professionals.

AI can optimize schedules, allocate resources, and even predict workflow bottlenecks based on historical data, significantly decreasing the need for project managers for repetitive tasks.

The answer for these professionals lies in adapting and evolving to more strategic functions. Over time, project managers' focus should shift to the ability to make data-driven decisions, manage the integration of AI into complex processes, and lead teams that utilize artificial intelligence to maximize organizational performance.

1.3   What you will gain along this journey.

By choosing to move to AI, you'll enter a dynamic field that not only values but requires continuous learning. Artificial intelligence is an ever-evolving field where discoveries and innovations are made daily.

This transition will allow you to develop a new professional mindset, based on adaptability and probabilistic reasoning.

Here are some of the key advantages you'll acquire along this journey:

1   Enhanced critical thinking.

The AI professional needs to develop the ability to analyze large volumes of data and identify patterns, which requires a critical and creative approach. The rigid logic of traditional software development gives way to an understanding of how algorithms "think" and adapt to data.

2   Powerful Tools at Your Disposal.

By learning AI, you'll have access to a number of tools that are revolutionary in their potential. From frameworks like TensorFlow and PyTorch to widely used programming languages like Python, the field of AI offers tools that enable the creation of complex solutions to global problems.

3   Greater professional impact.

One of the biggest advantages of becoming an AI expert is the ability to make a real impact in diverse industries. Whether you work with healthcare, education, or finance systems, AI allows you to develop solutions that can improve the lives of millions of people.

Take IBM's AI system, Watson, which is being used to help doctors diagnose and treat cancer patients. The ethical and social implications of this technology are profound, and being at the center of this revolution puts the professional in a role of global responsibility.

1.4   Challenges in the path of AI.

However, this transition is not without challenges. One of the biggest hurdles IT pros face when migrating to AI is the "learning curve."

The math and statistics behind machine learning algorithms may seem complex at first glance, especially to those who are used to traditional software development.

Additionally, AI requires a "test and learn" mindset, rather than the traditional "plan and build" approach that dominates IT development.

To overcome these challenges, it is essential to adopt a continuous learning posture. Today, there are a plethora of resources available to help with this transition, from online courses on platforms like Coursera and edX to attending hackathons and AI-focused conferences.

An example of how vital this continuous learning is can be seen in the trajectory of Andrew Ng, one of the most renowned AI scientists and co-founder of Coursera.

Ng began his career as a data scientist and, over time, has dedicated himself to the deep study of machine learning, launching one of the most popular and accessible courses on the topic. His example illustrates the importance of investing time and energy in mastering these new skills.

Additionally, the ability to collaborate with experts from different fields is key. AI, by its very nature, is interdisciplinary. An AI expert must not only understand programming, but also statistics, cognitive psychology, ethics, and even philosophy, to deal with the ethical and social dilemmas that AI raises.

2   Exploring the world of artificial intelligence.

Artificial intelligence (AI) is one of the most exciting and transformative areas of contemporary science and technology.

In simple terms, AI refers to the ability of computer systems to perform tasks that would normally require human intelligence. This includes activities such as reasoning, learning, perception, and even social interaction.

What makes AI especially powerful is its ability to process large amounts of data, identify patterns, and make predictions or make decisions based on those patterns, often faster and more accurately than humans.

Unlike traditional IT systems, which work on explicit rules and deterministic programming, AI, particularly in its machine learning branch, operates in a probabilistic manner. This means that instead of relying on a fixed set of instructions, AI systems are trained on data and learn to make decisions through the analysis of that data.

The more data they process, the more effective they become at accomplishing their tasks, adapting to new information, and improving their performance over time.

The field of AI encompasses several subdisciplines, such as machine learning, natural language processing (NLP), artificial neural networks, computer vision, and robotics.

Machine learning is undoubtedly one of the most important components of modern AI. It involves using algorithms to identify patterns in the data, and then, based on those patterns, predict outcomes or make classifications.

These algorithms can range from simple linear regression methods to sophisticated deep neural networks (deep learning), which excel at tasks that require understanding large volumes of complex data, such as speech and image recognition.

2.1   AI vs. IT: similarities, differences, and convergences.

For many IT professionals, the transition to AI may seem challenging at first glance, but the similarities between the two areas make this journey less intimidating.

Both AI and traditional IT deal with data manipulation and problem-solving through technology. The IT professional is already familiar with important concepts such as systems architecture, data management, and software development — all essential components for working with AI.

In fact, much of the knowledge that IT professionals already have is fundamental for the implementation of AI solutions in enterprise environments.

However, there are crucial differences. While traditional IT focuses on creating information systems based on explicit rules and manual programming, AI seeks a more autonomous and adaptive approach.

In IT, the behavior of the system is predefined by the programmer, who specifies each step of the software's operation. In AI, on the other hand, the system's behavior is determined by its ability to learn from the data provided.

This means that instead of creating rules, the AI developer creates models that can generalize and make decisions based on non-explicit patterns.

A clear example of this convergence can be seen in the area of network management. In the past, IT professionals have programmed specific rules to monitor network traffic and identify threats.

Today, AI systems can monitor entire networks in real time, automatically detect anomalies, and predict failures before they occur. In this case, technical knowledge in networking, fundamental for IT professionals, converges with machine learning skills to create smarter and more efficient solutions.

The convergence of AI and IT is becoming increasingly clear as tech companies adopt AI-powered automation solutions.

The field of DevOps, for example, is already being revolutionized by AI, which now helps automate the software development lifecycle, from automated testing to monitoring systems in production.

IT professionals who specialize in AI become a key player in this process, as they can leverage their expertise in infrastructure and programming while developing increasingly autonomous and intelligent systems.

2.2   Because AI is the natural next step for IT professionals.

The transition from IT to AI is not only a natural evolution, but a necessity for those who want to remain competitive in a rapidly changing technology landscape.

The reason why AI is the next logical step for IT professionals lies in the fact that technology is changing the role of traditional IT.

Market demands are increasingly focused on solutions that involve intelligent automation, predictive analytics, and operational efficiency, all areas where AI excels.

In recent years, the job market has come to value much more the professional who can transform large volumes of data into business value.

For this, skills in machine learning, predictive modeling, and data analysis are essential. Businesses across all industries are looking for ways to integrate AI into their decision-making processes, from marketing to operations to customer service.

According to McKinsey, companies that adopt AI effectively can increase their profit margins by up to 40% in just five years. This shows how the impact of AI goes beyond task automation: it is a complete transformation in the way companies operate.

IT professionals are already familiar with a variety of programming languages, data infrastructure, and operating systems. These skills are highly transferable to working with AI.

For example, the Python language, which is widely used by software developers, is also the primary language for machine learning.

Additionally, IT professionals who have experience with databases and big data systems find an advantage when working with AI, as most AI projects rely on well-structured and organized data.

An example that illustrates why AI is the natural next step for IT professionals can be seen in Netflix's trajectory.

Originally, Netflix was a DVD delivery company, but over the years, as the company has transformed into a digital streaming platform, AI has played a crucial role in its transition.

Netflix's recommendation algorithm is based on machine learning, analyzing users' preferences to suggest new content with a high level of personalization. This transformation of Netflix was possible because IT professionals within the company were prepared to integrate new AI skills into their existing infrastructure and software expertise.

In addition, the future of intelligent systems development depends on professionals who are able to unite the best of both worlds: the solid technical foundation of IT and advanced AI skills.

Career opportunities in this field are growing exponentially, with positions such as machine learning engineer, data scientist, and artificial intelligence specialist in high demand. For the IT professional, making this transition now means not only maintaining their relevance in the job market, but also positioning themselves as a leader in the future of technology.

By embracing AI, the IT professional not only adapts to the demands of the present, but prepares to shape the future.

3   Evaluating the starting point.

If you're an IT professional considering transitioning into the field of artificial intelligence (AI), know that much of the skills and knowledge you already have are essential and highly transferable to this new journey.

AI may seem like a complex and challenging field at first glance, but IT professionals bring with them a solid foundation of competencies that significantly ease this transition.

3.1   Programming logic and software development.

Programming logic is the backbone for both software development and the creation of AI systems. As an IT professional, you have already mastered programming languages such as Python, Java, or C++, which are also widely used in AI.

Python, in particular, is the most popular language for developing AI solutions, due to its simplicity and specialized libraries such as TensorFlow, PyTorch, Scikit-learn, and Keras.

His experience in software development gives him a valuable understanding of code structuring, debugging, and performance optimization.

These skills are essential for training machine learning models and building efficient data pipelines.

An example of how programming logic applies directly to the field of AI is the creation of algorithms for natural language processing (NLP).

To implement a solution that understands and generates human language, the developer needs to design logical flows that handle large volumes of text, identifying syntactic patterns and structures.

3.2   Data management.

AI algorithms rely fundamentally on data to "learn" and improve their predictions. As an IT professional, you're already familiar with managing large volumes of data—whether it's through relational databases like MySQL and PostgreSQL, or big data systems like Hadoop and Spark.

Knowledge of data architecture, modeling, and information extraction is crucial in training AI models, especially when it comes to organizing, cleaning, and preparing data for analysis.

One of the most common and critical tasks in AI development is data preprocessing. Before a model can be trained, the data needs to be structured correctly, which includes handling missing data, normalization, and removing outliers.

The experience you already have in data management is a substantial advantage, as it allows you to understand the complexities of dealing with large-scale data and ensure that it is ready to feed the AI algorithms.

3.3   Problem-solving and logical thinking.

IT professionals are, by nature, problem solvers. The entire software development process involves identifying requirements, understanding technical challenges, and creating practical and scalable solutions.

In the field of AI, this problem-solving skill is essential, as much of the work involves finding efficient ways to model and process data to solve complex issues.

For example, a machine learning engineer needs to address problems such as overfitting (when a model learns too much from training data, becoming unable to generalize to new data) or dealing with unbalanced datasets, in which one class of outcomes may be more prevalent than another.

The ability to break down these problems into smaller, approachable pieces, and apply specific techniques to fix them, is a straightforward skill that IT professionals bring to AI.

3.4   Automation and Scripting.

Automation is one of the most valuable skills an IT professional has ever mastered, and one that is highly applicable to AI development. Automation tasks, such as creating scripts to run repetitive processes, help streamline workflows within AI systems.

Additionally, automation is critical in the process of implementing machine learning pipelines that involve pre-processing data, training models, and deploying to production.

With familiarity in scripting, such as Bash or PowerShell, you can automate data collection and preprocessing, as well as create scripts that monitor and adjust AI models as the data changes over time.

Automation is also useful in tracking model performance metrics, helping to identify when adjustments or retraining are needed.

3.5   Infrastructure and Cloud Computing.

Implementing AI on a large scale often requires the use of distributed infrastructures and cloud computing. IT professionals, especially those with experience in system and network administration, already have the necessary knowledge to set up and maintain the infrastructure that will support the development and execution of AI models.

Cloud computing, offered by platforms such as AWS, Google Cloud, and Microsoft Azure, allows the training of models on machines with scalable computational capacity, which is crucial for training deep neural networks and processing large volumes of data.

Additionally, knowledge about DevOps and containers, such as Docker and Kubernetes, is highly valued in the field of AI, as these technologies enable the automation of model deployment in production environments and facilitate the scalability of AI-based solutions.

3.6   Information security and ethics.

Another strength of many IT professionals is their experience with information security, which is becoming increasingly relevant in the development of AI solutions.

Ethical concerns around data use and privacy are central to AI governance, and the need to maintain data integrity and security is paramount.

You already have the knowledge to ensure that the data used in AI models is protected from breaches and that it is used ethically and responsibly.

Data protection and compliance with regulations, such as the LGPD (General Data Protection Law) in Brazil or the GDPR in Europe, are areas that require the integration of cybersecurity with AI practices. Their familiarity with firewalls, encryption, and security protocols ensures that AI implementations are secure while minimizing risks associated with data vulnerability.

4   Skills you'll need to acquire.

While IT professionals have a solid foundation of knowledge that facilitates the transition to artificial intelligence (AI), there are several specialized skills that need to be acquired in order to achieve proficiency in this new field.

AI, especially machine learning and its branches, requires a unique combination of mathematical, technical, and conceptual skills.

These skills are crucial for the transition from an IT professional to an AI expert. While the learning curve can be steep, the job market for AI is filled with exciting opportunities for those who are willing to master these skills.

4.1   Advanced mathematics and statistics.

One of the first hurdles many IT professionals face when transitioning to AI is the need for a solid background in mathematics and statistics.

While programming is an important foundation, in-depth understanding of AI algorithms depends on fundamental mathematical concepts. AI is essentially a practical application of mathematical concepts that go beyond programming logic.

Linear algebra, for example, is a crucial area, especially in the context of neural networks. Matrices and vectors are the foundation of much of machine learning and deep learning.

When you train a deep learning model, you're essentially manipulating large matrices of weights and bias through a series of linear and nonlinear operations.

In addition, differential calculus plays a key role in adjusting the weights of machine learning models. The backpropagation technique, widely used in neural networks, relies on calculating derivatives to fit weights efficiently. Understanding basic calculus—such as derivatives, integrals, and gradients—is essential for anyone who wants to master training and optimizing AI models.

Statistics is another vital area of knowledge, as many of the AI algorithms rely on statistical concepts to process and interpret the data.

Terms such as probabilistic distributions, maximum likelihood estimates, and statistical inference become essential when building models that need to make predictions based on complex data.

Statistics is the basis of data analysis, and understanding concepts such as variance, standard deviation, correlation, and hypothesis tests is key to interpreting results from machine learning models and evaluating their effectiveness.

4.2   Theory and practice of machine learning.

While a basic understanding of algorithms may be sufficient in traditional IT, machine learning requires a detailed understanding of how different types of algorithms work and how to correctly apply them to specific problems.

Machine learning, at its core, involves algorithms that learn patterns from data and make predictions or classifications based on those patterns.

There are several types of machine learning, and each of them requires an understanding of its particularities:

1   Supervised learning: In this type of learning, you provide the algorithm with a set of labeled data so that it learns to map inputs to outputs.

Algorithms such as linear regression, decision trees, and support vector machines (SVM) fall into this category.

2   Unsupervised learning: Here, the data is not labeled, and the algorithm has to figure out patterns or groupings on its own. Methods such as clustering and principal component analysis (PCA) are common.

3   Reinforcement learning: A method inspired by behavioral psychology, where the AI agent learns to make decisions in a dynamic environment, maximizing rewards through trial and error.

This type of learning is widely used in robotics and games.

One of the first steps to acquiring this skill is to learn the fundamental principles of machine learning and the types of algorithms available.

This includes the ability to differentiate between using linear algorithms (such as regression) or more sophisticated methods (such as deep neural networks).

Platforms like Coursera and edX offer valuable introductory courses on machine learning that cover everything from basic concepts to more advanced techniques.

4.3   Deep learning and neural networks.

Deep learning is a subcategory of machine learning that has gained prominence for its impressive applications in computer vision, speech recognition, and natural language.

Unlike traditional machine learning algorithms, which often require the explicit definition of data characteristics, deep learning is based on artificial neural networks that "learn" these characteristics automatically from large volumes of data.

Artificial neural networks are inspired by the human brain, made up of artificial "neurons" that receive, process, and transmit information in a complex network.

Deep neural networks have multiple layers of neurons, which allows them to identify much more complex patterns in the data than traditional machine learning methods.

For an IT professional looking to move to AI, understanding how to build, train, and optimize neural networks is a key skill.

Frameworks like TensorFlow and PyTorch offer robust platforms for developing deep neural networks. These frameworks are widely used to build everything from simple classifiers to complex image recognition and natural language processing models.

Acquiring this skill involves learning how neural network layers work (convolutional layers, pooling layers, fully connected layers, etc.), how to adjust hyperparameters, and how to avoid problems such as overfitting, which occurs when a model fits too closely to the training data and fails to generalize to new data.

4.4   Data Manipulation and Analysis.

Data preparation and analysis are key activities in any AI project. Even if you have experience in databases, you will need to hone your data manipulation skills on a larger scale.

This includes data extraction, transformation, and loading (ETL) abilities, as well as pre-processing techniques such as normalization and missing data handling.

Tools such as Pandas and NumPy, in Python, are widely used for data manipulation in AI projects. These libraries allow you to organize, filter, and transform data efficiently, making it easy to feed models with data ready for analysis.

In addition to manipulating data, it is essential to acquire skills in data visualization to better understand the patterns that are being discovered by AI models.

Tools like Matplotlib and Seaborn are great for creating charts and visualizations that help interpret complex data and communicate findings clearly.

Data visualization plays an important role in both the data exploration process and the performance evaluation of models.

4.5   NLP (Natural Language Processing).

Natural Language Processing (NLP) is a subfield of AI that focuses on the interaction between computers and human language. NLP is essential for tasks such as chatbots, machine translation, and social media sentiment analysis. With the exponential growth of textual data, the ability to process, analyze, and interpret large volumes of text has become indispensable.

For an IT professional who wants to specialize in AI, learning NLP techniques is increasingly relevant. Tools such as spaCy and Natural Language Toolkit (NLTK) are popular libraries for manipulating text, entity extraction, and semantic analysis.

With NLP, you can train models to understand and generate natural language, opening doors to advanced applications such as virtual assistants and content recommendation systems.

4.6   Implementation and Deployment of AI Models.

Learning how to train AI models is one thing, but knowing how to deploy them in a production environment is another vital skill.

For models to be able to be used in real-world applications, it is necessary to ensure that they are scalable, fast, and secure in a production environment. This involves implementing machine learning pipelines that automate training and continuous model deployment.

Tools such as Docker and Kubernetes are widely used to scale and automate the deployment of models in production environments. Having a solid understanding of MLOps (Machine Learning Operations) will be crucial for professionals looking to integrate AI into already existing systems effectively and efficiently.

5   Defining your goals and interests within the field of AI.

As you begin your transition from an IT professional to the field of Artificial Intelligence (AI), one of the most important steps is to clearly define your goals and interests.

AI is a vast field, with several areas of expertise, each offering unique opportunities and requiring specific skill sets.

Before embarking on a journey of learning and career transformation, it's crucial to understand which path within AI you want to take and how your interests and skills can align with the needs of the market.

Setting clear objectives will help not only guide your learning trajectory, but also help you choose the right opportunities, the most suitable courses, and the areas that best match your professional and personal ambitions.

Defining your goals and interests is one of the most critical parts of your AI journey. With a clear plan and goals that align with your passions and the market, you'll be ready to explore the vast opportunities that AI offers and make a successful transition.

5.1 Self-knowledge: the first step to setting goals.

Before deciding which area of AI to pursue, it's essential to make an honest assessment of your skills, interests, and aspirations. What aspects of your IT experience give you the most satisfaction? What would you like to deepen or change?

For example, if you already work with large volumes of data and enjoy analytical tasks, perhaps machine learning or data science is the natural path.

On the other hand, if you have an interest in automation and interfaces, areas such as Natural Language Processing (NLP) or computer vision may be more appealing.

Ask questions like:

- What do I want to achieve with my transition to AI?
- Am I more interested in academic research or practical and commercial applications?
- Do I prefer to work with structured and numerical data, or am I more interested in language and images?
- Am I willing to lead projects or do I prefer to work in technical teams?

The answer to these questions will help you identify what type of AI professional you want to be. Being clear about your personal motivations will also help you stay focused during the inevitable challenges of this transition.

5.2 Exploring the main areas of AI expertise.

Artificial Intelligence encompasses several subareas, each with its own characteristics and applications. To define your interests, it is important to understand the main fields of AI activity.

Here are some of the most common and promising areas:

- Machine Learning. This is one of the most popular areas of AI, which focuses on developing algorithms that learn from data and make automated predictions or decisions.

  Machine learning is used in a variety of industries, including healthcare, finance, and technology, to predict patterns, identify trends, and automate decisions.

  If you enjoy working with data and have an affinity for mathematics and statistics, this could be a promising area for you.

- Deep Learning. A subfield of machine learning, deep learning uses deep neural networks to solve extremely complex problems, such as image recognition, speech, and autonomous driving.

  This area has seen explosive growth in recent years due to increased computing power and the availability of large data sets. Deep learning is ideal for those who want to work with more advanced and complex algorithms.

- Natural Language Processing (NLP). NLP is the field of AI that focuses on the interaction between computers and human language.

  NLP applications include automatic translators, chatbots, sentiment analysis, and voice assistants.

  If you have an interest in language and communication, NLP can be a fascinating field. Here, you will deal with understanding and generating text and speech, seeking to improve communication between humans and machines.

- Computer Vision. This area of AI is dedicated to teaching computers how to interpret and understand the visual world. Applications include image recognition, video analytics, and surveillance systems.

Professionals who are interested in images, videos, or the interaction between AI and the physical world can find great potential in this area.

- Robotics. For those interested in AI in physical applications, robotics combines hardware and software to create autonomous machines that can interact with the physical environment.

This area requires knowledge of programming, machine learning, and even control and mechanical engineering. Robotics is revolutionizing industries such as manufacturing, logistics, and healthcare.

- Ethics in AI and Governance. As AI becomes more widespread, there is an urgent need for professionals who understand the ethical implications and governance challenges associated with these technologies.

If you are concerned about issues of privacy, fairness, transparency, and accountability in the use of AI, this can be an interesting area to develop research or work in consulting and regulation.

5.3   Matching your interests with market demands.

Once you have a clear idea of the areas of AI that interest you most, the next step is to align those interests with market demands.

While it's important to pursue an area that you really enjoy, it's also prudent to look at the growth and job opportunities in each industry.

For example, according to a recent LinkedIn report, the demand for machine learning engineers and data scientists is growing rapidly, and many companies are competing for skilled talent.

Industries such as healthcare, finance, retail, and even entertainment are investing heavily in AI to enhance their operations and generate new insights.

Here are some questions you should consider when aligning your interests with market demands:

- Which industries are adopting AI the fastest?

- What types of specific skills are being most in demand in job offers?

- Are there certifications or courses that can add value to my profile and differentiate me in the market?

- Which industries are undergoing a digital transformation where AI will play a central role?

Often, the hottest areas of AI, such as machine learning, deep learning, and NLP, are in great demand in industries ranging from tech companies to financial institutions and biotech startups.

On the other hand, emerging sectors such as AI ethics and governance are growing in importance as concerns about privacy and algorithmic bias gain prominence.

5.4   Short, medium and long-term goals.

To ensure a successful transition, it is essential to set short, medium, and long-term goals. This includes everything from learning new skills to gaining more advanced positions in the job market.

- Short-term (3 to 6 months). During this period, your focus should be on developing the necessary technical skills. This can include learning specific programming languages (such as Python), understanding the fundamentals of machine learning, and working on hands-on projects that showcase your new competencies.

Take online courses and obtain relevant certifications that are recognized by the market.

Medium-term (6 to 18 months). Here, your focus will be on applying what you have learned in more challenging contexts. This could include participating in machine learning competitions, hackathons, or contributing to open-source projects.

- Another important goal for this period is to start building a solid portfolio, including hands-on projects that demonstrate your AI skills.

- Long-term (18 months or more). Once you've consolidated your knowledge, you can start pursuing more advanced opportunities, such as leadership roles in AI projects or even starting a transition to academic research.

Along this path, continue to hone your skills, explore new sub-fields of AI, or contribute to the ethical and responsible development of the technology.

5.5   Practical tips for defining your goals.

- Conduct an ongoing assessment of the market: Staying up-to-date on AI trends and demands will help you adjust your goals as needed.

- Build a practical portfolio: As you learn, work on concrete projects that can be displayed as proof of your skills.

- Seek mentorship: Talking to experts in the field can help you identify opportunities and paths that you have not yet considered.

6 Ideal learning path.

As you embark on the transition from IT professional to Artificial Intelligence (AI) specialist, it is critical to understand the key technologies and concepts that make up the vast AI ecosystem.

These pillars form the basis of their learning and are essential for creating solutions that can transform everything from business processes to people's daily lives.

6.1 Machine Learning: The Heart of Modern AI.

Machine Learning is undoubtedly the core of the AI revolution. It is an approach in which computer systems learn from data, adjusting their parameters automatically to improve performance in a specific task.

Unlike traditional programming methods, which require explicit instructions, machine learning algorithms can analyze large volumes of data, identify patterns, and make predictions based on those patterns.

There are three main types of machine learning:

1 Supervised learning.

In this type, the model is trained on labeled data—that is, each input has a known associated output. The model learns to map the inputs to the correct outputs.

Common examples include linear regression (used to predict ongoing values, such as home prices) and classification (used to categorize data into different classes, such as spam detection in emails).

2 Unsupervised learning.

Here, the model works with data that doesn't have labels. The goal is to find hidden patterns or groupings in the data.

Algorithms such as K-means and Principal Component Analysis (PCA) are often used for tasks such as grouping customers based on purchasing behavior or reducing dimensionality in complex data sets.

3   Reinforcement learning.

This method involves training an AI agent to make decisions in a dynamic environment, seeking to maximize rewards over time.

Reinforcement learning is widely used in robotics and games, being the basis for advances in game intelligence, such as the famous AlphaGo, developed by DeepMind, which defeated the world champion of Go.

For the IT professional who wants to specialize in AI, Machine Learning is the most natural starting point. Your familiarity with data structures and algorithms will allow you to quickly understand how machine learning models are trained and applied.

Popular tools such as Scikit-learn (Python) make it easy to develop and deploy these models, allowing you to experiment with different approaches quickly.

6.2   Deep Learning: The Next Frontier.

While machine learning focuses on algorithms that learn from data, deep learning takes this approach to a more advanced level.

Deep Learning is a subfield of machine learning that uses artificial neural networks, inspired by the functioning of the human brain, to process data in layers.

Deep neural networks consist of multiple layers of artificial neurons. Each layer learns a different representation of the data, allowing the model to solve complex problems with great accuracy.

Convolutional neural networks (CNNs), for example, are widely used for image recognition, while recurrent neural networks (RNNs) are effective at processing sequential data, such as time series or natural language.

Deep Learning has gained prominence due to its ability to handle tasks that require a high degree of complexity, such as facial recognition, machine translation, and even autonomous driving.

One of the biggest successes of deep learning has been the use of convolutional neural networks (CNN) in image recognition competitions, where these networks have significantly outperformed all previous approaches.

Tools such as TensorFlow and PyTorch have become the industry standard for developing deep learning solutions. These frameworks provide high-level libraries that make it easy to build, train, and deploy deep neural networks.

Mastering Deep Learning will allow you to solve highly complex problems and participate in innovative projects that are at the forefront of technology.

6.3 Natural Language Processing (NLP).

Natural Language Processing (NLP) is a subfield of AI dedicated to the interaction between computers and human language. NLP is critical for any application that requires text comprehension or generation, such as virtual assistants, chatbots, and sentiment analysis.

NLP encompasses various techniques and algorithms for understanding and manipulating language. Models such as Bag of Words (BoW) and TF-IDF help transform text into numerical data for analysis, while more advanced methods such as Word Embeddings (including Word2Vec and GloVe) are used to capture complex semantic relationships between words.

Recently, Transformers-based language models, such as the famous BERT (Bidirectional Encoder Representations from Transformers) and GPT-3, have revolutionized the field of NLP. These models, which use deep learning, are able to generate and interpret text with an almost human-like level of fluency.

For IT professionals, mastering NLP opens doors to the development of tools such as chatbots, virtual assistants (such as Alexa or Siri), or even advanced search and content recommendation engines.

6.4 Computer Vision.

Computer Vision is another subfield of AI that deals with the interpretation and analysis of visual data, such as images and videos.

Using deep learning techniques, computer vision enables AI systems to recognize objects, detect faces, track motion, and more.

Convolutional neural networks (CNNs) are widely used for computer vision tasks. Companies like Tesla and Waymo use these techniques in their autonomous driving systems, while Google Photos applies image recognition to automatically classify and organize users' photos.

Computer vision has a wide range of applications, ranging from security (facial recognition) to medical diagnosis (analysis of radiography images).

With the increasingly frequent use of image sensors and cameras, the demand for computer vision specialists continues to grow, making it a strategic area for AI professionals.

6.5   Generative Networks (GANs).

Adversarial Generative Networks (GANs) are an innovative technology that has been used to generate synthetic data, from images to text. GANs consist of two neural models that compete with each other: the generator, which creates new examples, and the discriminator, which tries to distinguish between real and generated examples. The interaction between these two networks leads the generator to create increasingly realistic data.

One of the most famous examples of GANs is applications that generate faces of people that don't exist, creating synthetic images that are virtually indistinguishable from the real thing.

GANs are also used to improve the quality of low-resolution images, generate digital art, and even design medicines.

Mastering GANs can be highly valuable for AI professionals working on creative projects or areas where synthetic data generation is essential, such as in gaming, art, or design.

6.6   AI Tools and Frameworks

In addition to the aforementioned concepts and techniques, it is crucial for IT professionals moving to AI to familiarize themselves with the tools and frameworks that facilitate the development and implementation of AI solutions.

Some of the key frameworks and libraries include:

- TensorFlow: Developed by Google, it is one of the most popular libraries for deep learning and machine learning.

- PyTorch: Loved by the research community, PyTorch offers great flexibility and is widely used in research and production projects.

- Keras: A high-level API that runs on top of TensorFlow and makes it easy to build neural networks.

- Scikit-learn: ideal for traditional machine learning, it offers a wide range of classification, regression, and clustering algorithms.

- OpenCV: computer vision library with support for a wide range of image processing algorithms.

These technologies and concepts form the foundation of any AI learning path.

By mastering them, you'll be equipped to meet the challenges of the AI field, develop innovative solutions, and open up new career opportunities.

Whether your interests are in machine learning, deep learning, NLP, or computer vision, these tools and concepts are the starting point for any IT professional looking to become an AI expert.

6.7   Programming Tools and Languages for AI

One of the key steps in the transition to the field of Artificial Intelligence (AI) is to become familiar with the most commonly used programming tools and languages.

These tools allow the development, training, and implementation of AI models in an efficient manner, as well as facilitate the creation of robust solutions in various applications.

By mastering these tools and programming languages, you'll be equipped to meet the challenges of AI and build robust solutions that meet the needs of a wide range of industries.

6.7.1 Python: The Preferred Programming Language for AI

The first and most important language you'll need to master in order to work with AI is undoubtedly Python.

This language has become widely adopted in the AI community due to its simplicity, versatility, and most importantly, the vast amount of specialized libraries available for machine learning, deep learning, natural language processing, and data science.

Why Python?

- Simplicity and readability. Python is known for its clear and easy-to-learn syntax, which allows developers to focus on the problems to be solved, without worrying about the complexity of the language. This makes the development of AI and machine learning algorithms more agile.

- Extensive library of tools. Python offers a vast array of libraries and frameworks dedicated to AI, which makes it easy to develop and train models. Libraries such as TensorFlow, PyTorch, Keras, and Scikit-learn are some of the most well-known examples.

6.7.2 Essential libraries and frameworks in Python.

- TensorFlow. Created by Google, TensorFlow is one of the most popular libraries for deep learning and machine learning. It enables developers to build and train complex neural networks and deploy AI models at scale, including for mobile devices.

- Keras. Initially a high-level API built on top of TensorFlow, Keras is a tool that simplifies building neural networks. It is ideal for deep learning beginners due to its ease of use and integration with TensorFlow.

- PyTorch. Popular among researchers, PyTorch, developed by Facebook, is known for its flexibility and support for research projects that require rapid iterations. It is widely used for deep learning experimentation, with a more dynamic approach than TensorFlow.

- Scikit-learn. For traditional machine learning, Scikit-learn is an essential library. It offers a wide range of classification, regression, and clustering algorithms, as well as tools for cross-validation, data processing, and feature selection.

- Pandas and NumPy. These libraries are essential for data manipulation and analysis in Python. NumPy supports operations with multidimensional arrays, while Pandas allows you to handle large volumes of data efficiently, using frameworks such as DataFrames, which make it easy to prepare data for AI models.

- Matplotlib and Seaborn. To visualize data, these libraries are essential. They allow the creation of rich graphs and visualizations, useful for analyzing model results and presenting findings.

Practical Tip:

If you're starting your journey in AI, Python should be your starting point. In addition to the above-mentioned libraries, there are numerous courses and tutorials available online that can help you learn Python for AI, from the basics to advanced projects.

6.7.3   A: Focused on Statistics and Data Science

While Python is preferred for AI, R is also a popular language, especially in the field of data science and statistical analysis.

The R language is widely used in universities and academic research due to its strong statistical capabilities and its libraries focused on data analysis.

Key Advantages of R:

- Statistical Power. R offers a wide range of statistical packages and functions that facilitate advanced data analysis. If you're interested in in-depth statistical analysis in AI, R can be an excellent tool.

- Data Visualization. R is known for its advanced visualization libraries, such as ggplot2, which allows you to create high-quality graphs and interactive visualizations, which are essential for analysis and communication of AI results.

However, due to its higher complexity compared to Python, and its lack of integration with advanced deep learning frameworks, R is generally less used for AI. It's more common in pure data science or deeper statistical analysis.

Practical Tip:

If you already have experience with R due to your background in statistics or data science, you may want to consider supplementing your education with Python, so that you have access to more comprehensive tools in the field of AI.

6.7.4 Java and C++: performance and integration with complex systems.

While Python is the dominant choice, Java and C++ still play important roles in the development of AI solutions, especially in systems that require high performance and integration with existing infrastructure.

6.7.5 Java.

Java is widely used in the development of enterprise AI solutions, due to its portability, security, and scalability. Companies that already have complex Java-based systems may prefer to maintain the integration of AI within this ecosystem.

Weka: Weka is a machine learning library in Java that offers tools for predictive modeling, data analysis, and data mining.

6.7.6 C++.

C++ is known for its top-notch performance and is widely used in AI to develop solutions that require real-time processing, such as robotics, computer vision, and embedded systems.

OpenCV: OpenCV is a computer vision library developed in C++ (also compatible with Python), widely used for applications that require fast image and video processing.

Practical Tip:

If you're working in a high-performance environment or need to integrate AI with complex software systems, Java or C++ may be a better fit for your projects. However, for most beginner AI professionals, Python remains the most flexible and affordable choice.

6.7.7   Tools for model training and deployment.

In addition to programming languages, there are several tools that facilitate the development and implementation of large-scale AI solutions.

Some of the key tools include:

• Jupyter Notebooks: One of the most popular tools for AI development, Jupyter Notebooks allow you to write and execute code in real-time, interspersed with text explanations and visualizations.

  They are widely used for experimentation in machine learning as they make it easier to document the development process.

• Google Colab: A cloud-based version of Jupyter Notebooks, Google Colab offers free GPUs so developers can train deep learning models without needing expensive hardware.

• Docker: Docker is a tool that enables the creation of containers to ensure that AI models are deployed in production environments with all the necessary dependencies.

  Docker is essential for the development of MLOps (Machine Learning Operations), which ensures the scalability and robustness of AI solutions in production environments.

• Kubernetes: To scale AI models across large IT infrastructures, Kubernetes is widely used to orchestrate containers. It automates the management, scalability, and operation of containers, ensuring that AI solutions can be efficiently distributed across multiple machines.

Practical Tip:

To streamline your workflow and ensure your projects can scale properly, invest time in learning Docker and Kubernetes. These tools are essential when you start developing large-scale AI solutions for production environments.

6.7.8   Cloud computing tools.

Much of the development of AI currently takes place on cloud computing platforms, which offer the flexibility and processing power needed to train models on large volumes of data.

Some of the top platforms include:

- Amazon Web Services (AWS). AWS SageMaker provides a complete solution for developing, training, and deploying machine learning models in the cloud.

- Google Cloud AI. Google Cloud offers a variety of AI tools, including AI Platform, which allows you to develop and train models with TensorFlow and other frameworks.

- Microsoft Azure AI. The Azure AI platform includes tools for machine learning, computer vision, natural language processing, and other AI solutions and is widely used in enterprise environments.

Practical Tip:

If you plan to work with AI on commercial projects or those that require scalability, learning how to use cloud platforms like AWS, Google Cloud, or Azure is an essential skill.

They allow you to train models on large data sets without the need to invest in expensive hardware.

6.8   Recommended courses and certifications to accelerate your transition

The transition of an IT professional to the area of Artificial Intelligence (AI) requires more than mastery of programming languages and tools; it also requires a formal and practical education in the main concepts of AI.

Fortunately, there is a wide range of courses and certifications. available online, created by both academic institutions and industry-leading companies, that can accelerate your journey and validate your new skills in the job market.

6.8.1   Machine Learning – Stanford University (Coursera).

This course is widely considered to be the best introduction to machine learning. Available online and taught by Andrew Ng, one of the leading experts in the field.

The course, offered by Stanford University through the Coursera platform, covers the fundamentals of machine learning and offers a solid foundation for professionals just starting out.

What you'll learn:

- Key concepts such as linear regression, logistic regression, neural networks and vector support...

- Supervised and unsupervised algorithms.

- Model optimization and tuning techniques.

Why it's important:

This course is extremely popular, having trained thousands of AI professionals around the world.

It is ideal for IT professionals who need a robust introduction to machine learning and want to understand what is behind the algorithms used in real projects.

Duration.: 11 weeks.

Certification: Yes.

Platform: Coursera.

6.8.2   Deep Learning Specialization – DeepLearning.AI (Coursera).

This specialization is another creation of Andrew Ng, through DeepLearning.AI, and is made up of five courses focused exclusively on deep learning. If you want to delve deeper into deep neural networks, this is the right course for you.

What you'll learn:

- Fundamentals of neural networks, backpropagation and activation functions.
- Convolutional neural networks (CNNs) for image processing.
- Recurrent neural networks (RNNs) and LSTMs for time series and NLP.
- Implementation of projects with TensorFlow and Keras.

Why it's important:

Deep learning is at the forefront of AI being used in cutting-edge applications such as image recognition, voice, and natural language processing. This specialization not only teaches you how to build neural networks but also how to apply them in real-world projects.

Duration: 3 to 6 months.

Certification: Yes.

Platform: Coursera.

6.8.3   AI for Everyone – DeepLearning.AI (Coursera).

Also created by Andrew Ng, AI for Everyone is a short, introductory course on the fundamental concepts of artificial intelligence, aimed at non-technical or entry-level professionals who want to understand the impact of AI on business and society.

What you'll learn:

- What is AI and how can it be applied in different industries.

- How to build an AI strategy for your organization.

- Understanding machine learning and deep learning algorithms, explained in an accessible way.

Why it's important:

If you are at the beginning of your transition and want to understand the overview of AI and its applicability in various industries, this course provides an excellent introduction.

It is ideal for professionals who want to discuss AI at a strategic or managerial level.

Duration: 4 weeks.

Certification: Yes.

Platform: Coursera.

6.8.4 Professional Certificate in Machine Learning and Artificial Intelligence – edX (Columbia University).

This professional certificate offered by Columbia University, one of the most renowned universities in the world, is aimed at professionals who want to acquire in-depth knowledge in machine learning and artificial intelligence.

What you'll learn:

- Fundamentals of machine learning and AI, including probabilistic models and unsupervised learning.

- Practical applications in computer vision, NLP, and robotics.

- How to implement AI algorithms at scale using advanced tools.

Why it's important:

This certificate is highly recognized in the market and offers a dense, practice-oriented curriculum with a focus on real-world applications. ~

For IT professionals who want a formal and in-depth qualification, this programme is an excellent choice.

Duration: 1 year (8 to 10 hours per week).

Certification: Yes.

Platform: edX.

6.8.5 AI Engineer Professional Certificate – IBM (Coursera).

IBM offers a professional certification aimed specifically at those who want to become AI engineers. The course includes a practical overview of building and implementing AI solutions in the corporate environment.

What you'll learn:

- Fundamentals of machine learning and deep learning.

- Development of models with Scikit-learn, TensorFlow and Keras.

- Implementing AI with IBM Watson APIs, such as natural language processing and sentiment analysis.

- Using AI in the cloud with IBM Cloud and Docker.

Why it's important:

This professional certificate is ideal for those who want to earn a certification recognized by the business sector, especially in enterprise AI solutions.

It provides hands-on experience with IBM's APIs and cloud tools that are widely used in technology companies.

Duration: 6 months (12 hours per week).

Certification: Yes.

Platform: Coursera.

6.8.6   Google Cloud AI & Machine Learning Professional Certificate (Google Cloud).

Google Cloud offers a professional certification that teaches participants how to use Google Cloud's infrastructure to develop, train, and deploy AI and machine learning models.

What you'll learn:

- Machine learning and deep learning fundamentals with native Google Cloud tools.

- How to use Google AI Platform, TensorFlow, and AutoML to build models.

- Integrating AI into enterprise solutions using Google's cloud infrastructure.

Why it's important:

If you want to integrate AI and machine learning into the enterprise environment, especially at scale, this certification gives you the opportunity to learn directly from Google Cloud.

It's especially useful for IT professionals who already work with cloud or enterprise infrastructure and want to add AI to their skill set.

Duration: 3 to 6 months

Certification: Yes

Platform: Google Cloud / Coursera

6.8.7   Microsoft Certified: Azure AI Engineer Associate.

If you're already working with Azure, Microsoft's cloud platform, this certification is ideal for learning how to develop, train, and deploy AI models using Azure AI services such as Azure Cognitive Services and Azure Machine Learning.

What you'll learn:

- Develop AI solutions using Azure Cognitive Services, Azure Bot Services, and Azure Machine Learning.

- Manage data for machine learning and train models on Azure infrastructure.

- Implementation of AI solutions at enterprise scale.

Why it's important:

This certification is aimed at AI engineers who want to build solutions with the Azure platform. It's an excellent choice for IT professionals who already have experience with Microsoft infrastructure and want to integrate AI into their corporate operations.

Duration: Varies according to previous experience.

Certification: Yes.

Platform: Microsoft Learn.

6.8.8   Practical tips for choosing a course or certification.

When choosing a course or certification, consider the following points:

- Experience level: If you're just starting your transition to AI, an introductory course like Stanford's "Machine Learning" is ideal. If you already have some experience and want to go deeper, look for specializations such as Deep Learning or more advanced professional certificates.

- Validity in the market: certifications from companies such as IBM, Google, Microsoft, and renowned universities are highly valued by the market. Choosing a course from one of these institutions can increase your professional credibility.

- Continuous learning: The field of AI is constantly evolving. Even after completing a certification, it's important to keep learning and experimenting with new algorithms and technologies.

These courses and certifications give you a strong foundation to develop your career in AI and will provide you with the practical and theoretical skills you need to excel in this competitive field.

7 Challenges and Obstacles on the Way: Overcoming the Technical Learning Curve

Artificial intelligence, with its complexity and constant evolution, presents a steep learning curve, even for tech-savvy professionals.

In this chapter, we will explore the key challenges and obstacles encountered in the AI learning process, as well as strategies for overcoming them.

7.1 Common challenges.

- Mathematical complexity. Many AI algorithms rely on advanced mathematical concepts such as calculus, linear algebra, and statistics. This barrier can be intimidating for those who do not have a solid background in mathematics.

- Large volume of information. The field of AI is constantly evolving, with new research and tools being developed daily. Keeping up with this evolution and staying up to date can be challenging.

- Lack of data. The quality and quantity of data are crucial for training AI models. Collecting and preparing data can be a time-consuming and labor-intensive process.

- Specialized hardware. Some AI algorithms, especially those involving deep learning, require specialized hardware such as GPUs, which can be expensive and inaccessible to many.

- Interpretability. AI models, especially deep neural networks, can be difficult to interpret, which makes it difficult to identify errors and debug.

Strategies to overcome the learning curve.

- Start with the basics. Start your studies with fundamental concepts of programming, statistics, and linear algebra.

- Utilize online resources. There are several online platforms, such as Coursera, edX, and Udemy, that offer both free and paid courses on AI.

- Join communities. Participating in forums, discussion groups, and online communities about AI allows you to exchange knowledge with other enthusiasts and professionals in the field.

- Experiment with hands-on projects. The best way to learn is by doing. Create simple projects to apply the concepts you've learned.

- Stay up to date. Keep up with the latest research and trends in the field through scientific articles, blogs, and events.

- Collaborate with other professionals. Working in a team can speed up the learning process and allow you to learn from the experience of others.

- Use tools and libraries. There are several open-source tools and libraries that make it easy to develop AI projects, such as TensorFlow, PyTorch, and Scikit-learn.

7.2   Additional Tips.

- Be patient. Learning AI takes time and dedication. Do not be discouraged by the initial difficulties.

- Break down your goals into smaller goals. Break down your learning goals into smaller, more achievable goals.

- Don't be afraid to make mistakes. Error is an integral part of the learning process.

- Seek mentorship. An experienced mentor can provide guidance and support during your learning journey.

By overcoming the challenges and obstacles, you will be well-prepared to explore the diverse opportunities that artificial intelligence offers.

7.3   Exploring the strategies to overcome the learning curve in AI in more depth

1   Start with the basics:

- Fundamentals of programming. Mastering a programming language like Python, which is widely used in AI, is critical.

- Mathematics. Solid knowledge in calculus, linear algebra, and statistics are essential for understanding machine learning algorithms.

- Concepts of statistics. Statistics is the basis for most machine learning algorithms, especially for data analysis.

2   Utilize online resources:

- Teaching platforms. Platforms like Coursera, edX, Udemy, and Khan Academy offer a variety of free and paid courses on AI, from the fundamentals to advanced topics.

- Tutorials and documentation. The official documentation for libraries such as TensorFlow and PyTorch is an excellent resource for learning about the features and how to use them.

- Blogs and articles. Keep up with blogs and articles from AI experts to stay up-to-date on the latest trends and research.

3   Join communities:

- Forums. Platforms like Stack Overflow, Reddit, and Kaggle are great places to ask questions, share knowledge, and find solutions to problems.

- Study groups. Join online or in-person study groups to discuss AI topics with other learners.

- Hackathons. Participating in hackathons is a great way to put your knowledge into practice and collaborate on real projects.

4   Experiment with hands-on projects:

Simple projects. Start with simple projects, such as image classifiers or prediction models, to consolidate your knowledge.

Machine learning competitions. Platforms like Kaggle offer several competitions where you can apply your knowledge to real challenges and compete with other participants.

Personal projects. Develop personal projects that interest you to maintain motivation and curiosity.

5   Stay up to date:

Follow the publications. Read scientific articles in journals such as Nature, Science, and arXiv.

Subscribe to newsletters. Subscribe to newsletters from companies and research institutions that work with AI.

Attend conferences. Attending conferences and workshops is a great opportunity to learn about the latest news and network.

6   Collaborate with other professionals:

Find a mentor. An experienced mentor can provide valuable guidance and feedback.

Work on projects as a team. Collaborating with other professionals on AI projects can accelerate your learning and expand your knowledge.

7   Use tools and libraries:

Machine learning libraries. Use libraries such as TensorFlow, PyTorch, Scikit-learn, and Keras to accelerate the development of your models.

Visualization tools. Use data visualization tools to better understand your models and the data you're working with.

7.4   Additional Tips:

- Networking. Connect with other professionals in the field through platforms such as LinkedIn.

- Be patient. Learning AI takes time and dedication. Don't be discouraged by the challenges.

- Have fun. AI is a fascinating and ever-evolving field. Have fun exploring your possibilities!

7.5   Addressing internal and external resistance to AI.

The implementation of Artificial Intelligence (AI) in organizations often encounters resistance, both internally and externally. This resistance can be a significant obstacle to AI adoption and success.

7.5.1   Causes of resistance.

- Fear of unemployment: the automation of tasks through AI can generate the fear of job loss.

- Lack of trust: The complexity of AI and the lack of transparency in some algorithms can lead to distrust in the results.

- Costs: Implementing AI solutions can require significant investments in infrastructure, software, and training.

- Resistance to change: Resistance to change is a natural phenomenon in any organization and can manifest itself in different ways.

- Lack of skills: The lack of skilled professionals to develop and implement AI solutions can be an obstacle.

- Ethical concerns: Issues such as privacy, algorithmic bias, and the responsible use of AI can raise ethical concerns.

7.5.2   Strategies to overcome resistance.

1   Transparent communication:

- Education: Promote workshops and training to explain the benefits of AI and how it can improve the organization's processes and results.

- Transparency: Be transparent about the goals of AI implementation and how the data will be used.

2   Employee involvement:

- Participation: Involve employees in the decision-making process and implementation of AI.

- Co-creation: Create a co-creation environment where employees can contribute ideas and suggestions.

3   Income Statement:

- Pilot projects: Start with pilot projects to demonstrate the benefits of AI in a tangible way.

- Metrics: Set clear metrics to measure the success of projects and communicate results.

4   Fear management:

- Trust: Reassure employees that AI is not a threat, but rather a tool to increase efficiency and productivity.

- Retraining: Offer reskilling programs so that employees can acquire new skills and adapt to change.

5   Trust Building:

- Explainability: use explainable algorithms so that employees can understand how decisions are made.

- Audit: Implement auditing processes to ensure ethics and transparency in the use of AI.

6   Cost Management:

- Cost-benefit analysis: Conduct a detailed analysis of the costs and benefits of implementing AI.

- Gradual investment: Start with smaller, simpler projects to reduce risk and demonstrate return on investment.

7   Addressing external resistance:

- Marketing and communication: Utilize marketing campaigns to educate audiences about the benefits of AI and debunk myths.

- Partnerships: Collaborate with other businesses, universities, and research institutions to develop AI solutions and build trust.

- Regulation: Keep up with AI-related regulations and standards and adapt your designs to ensure compliance.

In summary, overcoming resistance to AI requires a multi-pronged approach that involves transparent communication, employee engagement, results demonstration, fear management, and trust-building.

By proactively addressing concerns and challenges, organizations can reap the benefits of AI and drive innovation.

7.6   Maintaining motivation and avoiding burnout in AI learning.

The learning journey of Artificial Intelligence can be both exciting and challenging. The steep learning curve, the constant evolution of the field, and the complexity of concepts can lead to frustration and burnout.

To maintain motivation and achieve success on this path, it is essential to adopt some strategies:

1   Set realistic goals and celebrate small wins:

- SMART Goals: Set specific, measurable, attainable, relevant, and time-bound goals.

- Debt in stages: Break down big goals into small tasks to make it easier to track progress.

- Celebrate every achievement: Recognize and celebrate every small victory, no matter how small.

2   Create a consistent study routine:

- Fixed time: Determine a specific time to study and try to stick to that routine.

- Suitable environment: Create a quiet and organized study space.

- Regular breaks: Take short breaks during studies to rest and avoid mental fatigue.

3   Explore Hands-On Projects:

- Real-world applications: Relate theoretical concepts to practical projects to visualize the impact of AI in the real world.

- Hackathons and competitions: Participate in hackathons and competitions to put your knowledge into practice and learn from others.

- Personal projects: develop projects that interest you to maintain intrinsic motivation.

4   Connect with the Community:

- Online forums and groups: Participate in forums and discussion groups to exchange ideas and ask questions.

- Events and meetups: Attend events and meetups to meet other professionals in the field and expand your network.

- Mentoring: Seek a mentor to guide you and offer support.

5   Take Care of Physical and Mental Health:

- Physical exercise: regular physical exercise helps reduce stress and improve concentration.

- Healthy eating: a balanced diet provides the energy needed for studies.

- Adequate sleep: get enough sleep to ensure good cognitive performance.

- Hobbies: Make time for activities you enjoy to relax and recharge.

6   Keep Curiosity:

- Explore new areas: Don't limit yourself to a single topic. Explore different areas of AI to expand your knowledge.

- Read articles and keep up with the news: Stay up-to-date on the latest research and trends.

7 Be patient and persistent:

- Continuous learning: AI is an ever-evolving field. Be prepared to learn continuously.

- Don't give up: Face challenges as opportunities for growth.

Note that the AI learning journey is a marathon, not a sprint. By staying motivated and adopting healthy habits, you will be better prepared to overcome challenges and achieve your goals.

7.7   Managing the fear of failure in AI learning.

The fear of failure is a common feeling for all of us, especially when we are learning something new and challenging like Artificial Intelligence.

Anxiety and insecurity can paralyze us and prevent us from reaching our full potential. However, there are several strategies we can use to overcome these feelings and stay motivated.

1   Understanding the Origin of Fear:

- Perception of complexity. AI can seem like a very complex and comprehensive field, which can generate the feeling that we are not capable of learning.

- Comparison with others. Comparing yourself to others who seem more advanced can generate feelings of inferiority.

- Fear of judgment: The fear of being judged for not understanding something or making mistakes can be paralyzing.

- Strategies for Overcoming Fear.

- Change your perspective. Instead of focusing on the fear of failure, focus on learning and personal growth. Every mistake is an opportunity to learn and improve.

- Start small. Break down your goals into smaller, more achievable goals. By celebrating every small victory, you'll gain confidence and motivation to keep going.

- Be kind to yourself. We all make mistakes. Be patient with yourself and learn from your experiences.

- Celebrate the process. Enjoy the learning journey, rather than focusing solely on the end result.

- Seek support. Share your challenges with friends, colleagues, or mentors. Having someone to talk to and offer support can make all the difference.

- Practice self-compassion. Be kind to yourself and recognize that you are doing your best.

- Visualize success. Imagine yourself achieving your goals. Visualization can boost your confidence and motivation.

- Keep a gratitude journal. Write down the things you are grateful for. This can help change your perspective and increase your positivity.

7.7.1 Practical Tips.

- Start with the basics. Master the fundamentals before moving on to more complex topics.

- Utilize online resources. There are several platforms and online communities that offer support and resources for learning.

- Participate in study groups. Sharing learning with others can help you feel more connected and motivated.

- Practice regularity. Study a little bit every day, instead of trying to learn everything at once.

- Take breaks. It is important to rest and recharge to maintain productivity.

7.8 Maintaining Motivation and Avoiding Burnout in AI Learning.

The learning journey of Artificial Intelligence can be both exciting and challenging. The steep learning curve, the constant evolution of the field, and the complexity of concepts can lead to frustration and burnout.

To maintain motivation and achieve success on this path, it is essential to adopt some strategies:

1   Set Realistic Goals and Celebrate Small Victories:

- SMART Goals: Set specific, measurable, attainable, relevant, and time-bound goals.

- Break it down into steps. Break down big goals into small tasks to make it easier to track progress.

- Celebrate every achievement. Recognize and celebrate every small victory, no matter how small.

2   Create a Consistent Study Routine.

- Fixed time. Determine a specific time to study and try to stick to that routine.

- Suitable environment. Create a quiet and organized study space.

- Regular breaks. Take short breaks during your studies to rest and avoid mental fatigue.

3   Explore hands-on projects.

- Real applications. Relate theoretical concepts to practical projects to visualize the impact of AI in the real world.

- Hackathons and competitions. Participate in hackathons and competitions to put your knowledge into practice and learn from others.

- Personal projects. Develop projects that interest you to maintain intrinsic motivation.

4 Connect with the Community.

- Online forums and groups. Participate in forums and discussion groups to exchange ideas and ask questions.

- Events and meetups. Attend events and meetups to meet other professionals in the field and expand your network.

- Mentoring. Seek a mentor to guide you and offer support.

5 Take Care of Physical and Mental Health.

- Physical exercises. Regular physical exercise helps reduce stress and improve concentration.

- Healthy eating. A balanced diet provides the energy needed for studies.

- Adequate sleep. Get enough sleep to ensure good cognitive performance.

- Hobbies. Make time for activities you enjoy to relax and recharge.

6 Stay curious.

Explore new areas: Don't limit yourself to a single topic. Explore different areas of AI to expand your knowledge.

Read articles and keep up with the news: Stay up-to-date on the latest research and trends.

7   Be patient and persistent.

Continuous learning: AI is an ever-evolving field. Be prepared to learn continuously.

Don't give up: face challenges as opportunities for growth.

Remember: The AI learning journey is a marathon, not a sprint. By staying motivated and adopting healthy habits, you will be better prepared to overcome challenges and achieve your goals.

7.9   Building a network of contacts in the field of AI: the key to success.

The importance of networking in the area of AI is undeniable. By connecting with other professionals, you not only expand your knowledge but also open doors to new opportunities for learning, collaboration, and professional growth.

Why is networking so important in AI?

- Knowledge sharing: By interacting with other professionals, you can learn about new techniques, tools, and trends in the field.

- Mentoring: Finding an experienced mentor can help you overcome challenges and accelerate your development.

- Project collaboration: Working on projects with other professionals can help you develop new skills and expand your knowledge.

- Job opportunities: Your network of contacts can help you find new job opportunities or projects.

- Visibility: By participating in events and communities, you increase your visibility in the job market.

How to build a network of contacts in the area of AI?

- Attend events: Conferences, meetups, hackathons, and workshops are excellent opportunities to meet other professionals in the field.

- Use online platforms: Platforms like LinkedIn, GitHub, and Kaggle are great tools for connecting with other professionals in the field.

- Join study groups: Joining study groups can help you meet like-minded people and learn together.

- Be active in online communities: Join forums and discussion groups, share your knowledge, and help others.

- Collaborate on open source projects: Contributing to open source projects is a great way to demonstrate your skills and meet other developers.

- Keep in touch: Don't limit yourself to just meeting new people. Stay in touch with your network, share your achievements, and offer help when possible.

Tips for building lasting relationships:

- Be genuine: Show genuine interest in people and their ideas.

- Offer help: Be willing to help others when you need it.

- Be a good listener: Listen carefully to what others have to say.

- Keep in Regular Contact: Send messages, emails, or call your contacts regularly.

In summary, investing in your network of contacts is an investment in your professional future. By building strong relationships with other AI professionals, you'll be better prepared to meet the challenges of the job market and achieve your goals.

8   Developing a Growth Mindset: Cultivating Continuous Learning.

A growth mindset is the belief that our skills and intelligence can be developed with effort and dedication.

Unlike the fixed mindset, which believes that our capabilities are innate and immutable, the growth mindset pushes us to seek new challenges, learn from mistakes, and continuously evolve.

Why is the growth mindset important in the AI area?

- AI is constantly evolving: new technologies and algorithms emerge all the time, requiring professionals to adapt and learn continuously.

- Complex problems require new solutions: Solving complex problems in the field of AI requires creativity and the ability to think outside the box.

- Collaboration is key: A growth mindset makes it easier to collaborate with other professionals, as it promotes openness to new ideas and perspectives.

How to cultivate a growth mindset?

- Embrace challenges: View challenges as opportunities for learning and growth, rather than obstacles.

- Celebrate the process: Enjoy the learning journey rather than just focusing on the end result.

- Value mistakes: see mistakes as opportunities for learning and improvement.

- Seek feedback: Solicit feedback from peers and mentors to identify areas for improvement.

- Stay curious: constantly ask yourself "how can I improve?" and "what else can I learn?".

- Surround yourself with inspiring people: Interact with people who share your desire to learn and grow.

- Practice self-compassion: Be kind to yourself and recognize your efforts.

- Visualize success: Imagine yourself achieving your goals. Visualization can boost your confidence and motivation.

- Read and get informed: Stay up-to-date on the latest trends and research in the field of AI.

- Try new things: Get out of your comfort zone and explore new areas of knowledge.

Practical strategies for everyday life:

- Study regularly: Take time each day to learn something new.

- Participate in online communities: interact with other professionals in the field and share your knowledge.

- Take courses and workshops: invest in your continuing education.

- Work on personal projects: apply your knowledge to hands-on projects.

- Keep a learning journal: Write down your progress and challenges.

In summary, cultivating a growth mindset is an ongoing journey. By adopting these strategies, you will be better prepared to face the challenges of the AI area and achieve your goals.

9 Dealing with burnout: how to avoid mental and physical burnout while learning.

Burnout is an increasingly common problem, especially in areas that require a high level of concentration and dedication, such as learning Artificial Intelligence.

Feelings of overwhelm, mental and physical exhaustion, and loss of motivation are common symptoms of burnout. To prevent this from happening, it is important to adopt some strategies:

9.1 Set boundaries.

- Time to start and end. Set specific times to study and respect them.

- Regular breaks. Take short breaks every hour to rest and stretch.

- Disconnect. Establish moments to completely disconnect from AI-related activities.

9.2 Create a Healthy Routine.

- Sleep. Get enough sleep to ensure your body and mind are rested.

- Feeding. Maintain a balanced diet for energy throughout the day.

- Exercises. The practice of physical activities helps to reduce stress and improve concentration.

9.3 Organize your Time.

- Time management. Use techniques such as the Pomodoro technique to optimize your studies.

- Prioritize tasks. Identify the most important tasks and focus on them first.

- Avoid procrastination. Create a distraction-free study environment.

9.4   Take Care of Mental Health.

- Meditation and mindfulness. Practice relaxation techniques to reduce stress.

- Hobbies. Make time for activities that you enjoy and that bring you pleasure.

- Seek support. Talk to friends, family, or a mental health professional about how you feel.

9.5   Vary the activities.

- Diversified routine. Alternate between different types of learning activities to avoid monotony.

- Explore different areas of AI. The breadth of AI allows you to explore diverse topics and maintain interest.

9.6   Be Realistic with Your Goals.

- Achievable goals. Set realistic goals and celebrate your achievements.

- Avoid comparison. Compare your progress to your own and not to that of others.

9.7   Recognize the Signs of Burnout.

- Fatigue. Excessive tiredness, both physical and mental.

- Demotivation. Loss of interest in activities.

- Difficulty concentrating. Difficulty concentrating on tasks.

- Social isolation. Tendency to isolate themselves and avoid social interactions.

If you notice that you are suffering from burnout, seek professional help. A therapist can help you develop strategies for dealing with stress and anxiety.

Remember: It's important to find a work-life balance. By taking care of your physical and mental health, you'll be better prepared to face the challenges of learning AI.

10 Creating a portfolio: Demonstrate your skills and stand out in the job market.

A portfolio is more than just a resume. It's a showcase of your skills, a space for you to show what you're capable of.

For professionals in the field of Artificial Intelligence (AI), a well-built portfolio can be the key to landing a dream job or a challenging project.

10.1   Why is a portfolio important?

- Hands-on demonstration: A portfolio allows you to showcase your skills in a hands-on way, through real projects.

- Differentiation: In an increasingly competitive job market, a well-designed portfolio helps you stand out.

- Credibility: Successful projects demonstrate your competence and experience.

- Communication: A well-structured portfolio makes it easier to communicate your skills and knowledge.

10.2   How to create an effective portfolio?

1. Define your audience: Who do you want to impress with your portfolio? Tailor content to suit your target audience.

2. Choose the format: Your portfolio can be a website, an interactive PDF, or an online platform like GitHub.

3. Select your best projects: Include only the projects that best demonstrate your skills and align with your career goals.

4. Create a narrative: tell a story with your projects. Show how you've evolved over time and what challenges you've overcome.

5. Use clear and concise language: Explain your projects clearly and objectively, avoiding technical jargon.

6. Include technical details: Describe the technologies, tools, and methodologies used in each project.

7. Use images and videos: Use images and videos to illustrate your projects and make them more interesting.

8. Highlight your results: show the results achieved with your projects, such as improving a process or creating a new product.

9. Be organized: Keep your portfolio organized and easy to navigate.

10. Keep it up to date: Update your portfolio regularly to include new projects and demonstrate your professional growth.

10.3   What to include in your portfolio?

• Personal projects: Projects that you have developed on your own.

• Academic projects: work carried out during undergraduate or graduate studies.

• Work projects: projects developed in previous companies.

• Hackathons and competitions: participation in events and competitions.

• Articles and publications: technical articles, blogs, or publications in specialized magazines.

• Certificates: certifications in courses and training.

Examples of platforms to create a portfolio:

- GitHub: Ideal for developers, it allows you to host your code and create pages for your projects.

- Kaggle: platform for data scientists, where you can share your notebooks and datasets.

- Wix, Squarespace: platforms for creating custom websites.

- Behance: platform to showcase creative work.

Extra tips:

- Ask for feedback: Ask friends, colleagues, and mentors to give feedback on your portfolio.

- Customize your portfolio: Tailor your portfolio for each job opportunity.

- Use keywords: Use keywords relevant to the AI area to make it easier to search for your portfolio.

Remember: Your portfolio is your showcase to the world. Invest time and effort in creating it to stand out in the job market.

11 Building a strategic portfolio in artificial intelligence: a guide to the selection of impactful projects.

In the current scenario of Artificial Intelligence, where technological evolution occurs at a rapid pace, building a differentiated portfolio has become a crucial element for professionals who want to excel in this field.

With the emergence of new AI tools, frameworks, and applications, strategic project selection has gained even more importance.

The alignment of projects with professional objectives transcends the simple demonstration of technical skills. In a market where 67% of employers are looking for professionals with hands-on experience in AI, it is critical to develop projects that reflect not only technical skills but also an in-depth understanding of the technology's impact on business.

Recent studies indicate that professionals with portfolios well aligned with market demands are 40% more likely to be hired.

11.1   Relevant aspects to consider.

Relevance to today's AI market must consider emerging trends such as:

- Natural Language Models (NLP) and practical applications.
- Computer vision and pattern recognition systems.
- Reinforcement learning in complex environments.
- Ethics and responsibility in AI.
- Optimization of resources and energy efficiency.
- Integration of AI with IoT and edge computing.
- Applications in specific sectors (health, finance, retail).

As for the complexity of the projects, strategic progression is key. Research shows that 82% of recruiters place a higher value on consistent evolution than complex projects in isolation.

A recommended approach includes:

1. Initial Projects:

- Implementation of classic machine learning algorithms.
- Exploratory data analysis with popular libraries.
- Development of basic chatbots.
- Image classification using pre-trained models.

2. Intermediate Projects:

- Personalized recommendation systems.
- Sentiment analysis on social networks.
- Real-time object detection.
- Time series forecasting.

3. Advanced Designs:

- Development of own deep learning models.
- Generative AI systems.
- Implementation of distributed AI architectures.
- Intelligent automation solutions.

Originality in AI projects has gained a new dimension with the popularization of tools such as GPT and DALL-E.

To stand out, professionals must:

- Develop solutions to unique or overlooked problems.
- Combine different technologies in an innovative way.
- Create differentiated user interfaces and experiences.
- Address relevant social or environmental issues.
- Implement significant improvements to existing solutions.

11.2   Technical aspects to consider.

With the constant emergence of new tools, frameworks, and methodologies in AI, technical excellence in portfolio construction has gained more complex and sophisticated dimensions.

It is not enough just to know algorithms and libraries; It is necessary to demonstrate mastery in aspects such as software architecture, sustainable development practices, and implementation of quality standards that meet the requirements of modern industry.

Recent surveys indicate that 92% of technical recruiters evaluate the quality of the code and the structuring of projects as decisive criteria in the selection process.

In a scenario where competition for positions in AI intensifies, attention to essential technical aspects becomes a crucial element to stand out in the market and build a solid career in this ever-evolving field.

Essential technical aspects for a modern AI portfolio:

1. Clear Documentation:

- Detailed description of the architecture.
- Explanation of technological choices.
- Performance metrics and results.
- Challenges encountered and solutions implemented.

2. Clean and Organized Code:

- Good programming practices.
- Proper versioning.
- Automated testing.
- Relevant inline documentation.

3. Reproducibility:

- Well-defined virtual environments.

- Clear installation instructions.
- Sample or simulated data.
- Automated configuration scripts.

Current trends to consider:

• Explainable AI (XAI):

- Transparency in the models.
- Interpretability of decisions.
- Analysis of bias and fairness.

• Green AI:

- Energy efficiency.
- Optimization of resources.
- Computational sustainability.

• MLOps:

- Pipeline automation.
- Model monitoring.
- Continuous integration.

To maximize portfolio impact:

1. Professional Presentation:

- Organized personal website.
- README.md well structured.
- Interactive demonstrations when possible.
- Visual documentation (diagrams, graphs).

2. Strategic Sharing:

- Active presence on GitHub.
- Technical articles on specialized blogs.

- Participation in AI communities.
- Presentations at technical events.

3. Constant Update:

- Incorporation of new technologies.
- Refinement of existing designs.
- Adaptation to market trends.
- Community Feedback

An effective AI portfolio should demonstrate not only technical competence, but also:

- Critical thinking in problem solving.
- Ability to adapt to new technologies.
- Understanding the business impact of solutions.
- Ethical awareness and social responsibility.
- Clear technical communication skills.

Note that building a portfolio in AI is a dynamic process that requires strategic planning, consistent execution, and constant adaptation to market changes.

With most companies planning to increase their investments in AI in the coming years, a well-built portfolio becomes a key competitive differentiator for professionals in the field.

11.3   Examples of projects.

In the rapidly evolving technological landscape, the strategic choice of Artificial Intelligence projects has become critical to building a differentiated portfolio.

With the exponential advancement of AI technologies and the growing demand for sophisticated solutions, it is essential to develop projects that demonstrate not only technical competence but also in-depth understanding of practical applications and business impact.

1   Computer Vision.

The field of computer vision is experiencing a revolution with the advent of transformers models and hybrid architectures.

Modern projects in this area include:

- Intelligent surveillance systems with anomalous behavior detection.
- Facial recognition with privacy by design.
- Medical diagnosis through radiological image analysis.
- Automated real-time industrial inspection.
- Analysis of urban traffic and mobility.
- Gesture recognition for natural interfaces.
- Responsive augmented reality systems.

Emerging technologies in this field include:

- Vision Transformers (ViT).
- Few-shot learning models.
- Efficient architectures for edge computing.
- 3D vision systems and point clouds.
- Multimodal sensor fusion.

2   Natural Language Processing (NLP).

With the emergence of models like GPT-4 and Claude, the field of NLP has significantly expanded its possibilities.

Relevant projects include:

- Specialized virtual assistants by industry.
- Intelligent summarization systems.
- Multimodal sentiment analysis.
- Chatbots with adaptive personality.
- Advanced contextual translation.
- Generation of personalized content.
- Analysis of legal documents.

3   Featured technologies and frameworks.

- Transformers with efficient attention.
- Zero-shot multilingual templates.
- Fine-tuning optimized frameworks.
- Knowledge grounding systems.
- Hybrid architectures with recovery.

4   Classic Machine Learning.

Even with the advancement of deep learning, classic machine learning remains relevant with critical applications:

- Real-time fraud detection systems.
- Dynamic pricing models.
- Supply chain optimization.
- Multivariate demand forecasting.
- Contextual recommendation systems.
- Predictive maintenance analytics.
- Advanced behavioral segmentation.

5   Modern techniques and tools:

- AutoML for hyperparameter optimization.
- Ensemble methods adaptativos.
- Automatic feature engineering.
- Interpretability and explainability.
- MLOps and continuous monitoring.

6   Deep Learning and Neural Networks.

The field of deep learning continues to expand with increasingly sophisticated architectures:

- Multimodal generative systems.
- Self-adaptive neural networks.
- Cross-modal attention models.
- Neural-symbolic architectures
- Optimized transfer learning
- Continuous learning systems.
- Quantum neural networks.

Recent technological innovations:

- Arquitecturas Neural Architecture Search.
- Energy efficiency models.
- Federated learning systems.
- Probabilistic neural networks.
- Specialized hardware for deep learning.
- AI applied to specific domains.

11.4   The application of AI in different sectors has generated highly impactful projects:

1. Health:

- Automatic diagnostic imaging.
- AI-assisted drug discovery.
- Prediction of epidemic outbreaks.
- Personalized medicine.
- Advanced genomic analysis.

2. Finance:

- Adaptive algorithmic trading.
- Real-time risk analysis.
- Money laundering detection.
- Contextual credit scoring.
- Automated financial advice.

3. Sustainability:

- Optimization of energy consumption.
- Smart environmental monitoring.
- Prediction of natural disasters.
- Precision agriculture.
- Water resources management.

4. Industry 4.0:

- Advanced predictive maintenance.
- Optimization of industrial processes.
- Automated quality control.
- Collaborative robotics.
- Intelligent digital twins.

11.5 Emerging trends to consider:

1 Explainable AI (XAI):

- Interpretability of models.
- Auditing decisions.
- Algorithmic bias analysis.

2 Green AI:

- Computational efficiency.
- Reduction of energy consumption.
- Algorithmic sustainability.

3 Edge AI:

- Distributed processing.
- Optimization for mobile devices.
- Privacy by design.

4 AI Ethics:

- Algorithmic governance.
- Privacy and security.
- Responsible social impact.

11.6 To maximize portfolio impact, it is essential to:

1. Professional Documentation:

- Clear description of objectives.
- Detailed methodology.
- Quantified results.
- Well commented code.

2. Impact Demonstration:

- Performance metrics.
- Practical use cases.
- Cost-benefit analysis.
- Scalability of the solution.

3. Responsible Innovation:

- Ethical considerations
- Environmental impact
- Accessibility
- Social inclusion

11.7   Fundamental Principles for the Development of Innovative Projects in AI.

The development of projects in Artificial Intelligence requires a multifaceted and strategic approach, based on essential principles that guarantee not only technical success, but also significant impact on the market and society.

In a scenario where 93% of companies consider AI as a strategic priority, adherence to these principles becomes crucial for the development of truly impactful solutions.

Relevance to the current market emerges as the first fundamental pillar. Recent research indicates that 87% of successful AI projects are those that respond directly to specific market needs.

This implies a deep understanding of technological trends, sectoral demands and market gaps. Developers must constantly stay up-to-date on the latest innovations and market requirements, ensuring that their solutions remain competitive and relevant.

The potential for scalability represents the second critical element. With the AI market projected to grow by 38% annually through 2030, scalable solutions become imperative.

The project's architecture must contemplate not only immediate needs, but also foresee future expansions, considering aspects such as cloud-native infrastructure, code modularity, and optimization of computational resources.

Originality in approach stands out as the third essential principle. In a field where 75% of solutions follow similar standards, innovation differentiates truly impactful projects.

This involves not only the implementation of unique algorithms, but also creative approaches to problem-solving, innovative combinations of existing technologies, and the development of intuitive and differentiated interfaces.

Technical quality is the fourth fundamental pillar. Studies show that 82% of AI projects fail due to technical deficiencies.

Technical excellence should permeate all phases of development, from initial architecture to final implementation, including robust documentation, comprehensive testing, clean code practices, and adherence to MLOps principles.

Finally, positive social impact emerges as the fifth crucial element. With 91% of consumers preferring companies that demonstrate social responsibility, AI projects must consider their impact on society. This includes aspects such as environmental sustainability, social inclusion, user privacy, and algorithmic ethics.

The integration of these five principles creates a solid framework for the development of AI projects that not only meet technical and market demands, but also contribute positively to technological and social advancement.

In an increasingly competitive and conscious market, adherence to these principles becomes a fundamental strategic differential for the lasting success of Artificial Intelligence projects.

Building a portfolio in AI requires a balanced mix of projects that demonstrate both technical proficiency and understanding of market needs.

11.8   Applying AI to real problems: practical examples.

Applying AI to real problems is the best way to demonstrate your ability to solve problems and create value.

Some practical examples include:

1   Healthcare: development of models for diagnosing diseases, analyzing medical images, creating virtual assistants for patients, etc.

2   Finance: creation of fraud detection systems, credit analysis, investment recommendations, etc.

3   Marketing: developing product recommendation systems, analyzing customer sentiments, creating personalized marketing campaigns, etc.

4   Environment: monitoring natural disasters, predicting climate change, optimizing energy consumption, etc.

11.9   How to collaborate and learn from the AI community.

The AI community is vast and collaborative. By connecting with other professionals, you can learn new techniques, find mentors, and collaborate on projects.

Some ways to engage with the community include:

- Participate in online forums and groups: Platforms like Stack Overflow, Kaggle, and GitHub are great for asking questions, sharing knowledge, and collaborating on projects.

- Participate in hackathons and competitions: These events are a great opportunity to put your knowledge into practice and meet other professionals.

- Contribute to open source projects: Collaborating on open source projects allows you to learn from other developers and hone your skills.

- Attend meetups and conferences: These events are a great way to connect with other professionals in your field and learn about the latest trends.

Tips for collaborating with the community:

- Be proactive: offer your help and collaborate on projects.
- Be respectful: Respect the opinions of others and be open to criticism.
- Share your knowledge: Help other community members with their questions.

By following these tips and engaging with the AI community, you'll build a solid network of contacts and continuously learn.

12 Building your personal brand: Develop your professional identity and stand out in the job market.

Building a personal brand is essential to stand out in the increasingly competitive job market. Your personal brand is your professional identity, the perception that others have of you and what you represent.

By building a strong brand, you increase your chances of landing opportunities, building lasting relationships, and achieving success in your career.

12.1   Why build a personal brand?

In today's professional landscape, marked by hyperconnectivity and accelerated digital transformation, building a personal brand has become not only a competitive advantage, but a fundamental necessity for professional success.

With the advancement of social networks, artificial intelligence, and new ways of working, the way we present ourselves and position ourselves in the market has undergone a significant revolution.

Professional differentiation, the first pillar of personal branding, has gained a new dimension with the expansion of remote and hybrid work. In a global market where professionals from different countries compete for the same opportunities, having a well-defined and authentic personal brand has become a crucial differentiator.

It's not just about standing out from the local competition, but about creating a unique digital presence that resonates globally.

Credibility, the second fundamental element, plays an even more relevant role in the era of disinformation.

A strong personal brand acts as a seal of trust, especially important when we consider that 92% of recruiters, according to recent research, consult candidates' professional social networks before making hiring decisions.

Building authority through relevant content, participation in industry events, and meaningful contributions to the professional community has become an essential avenue for establishing lasting credibility.

Networking, the third crucial aspect, has been radically transformed with digital platforms. Professional connections today transcend geographical barriers, allowing for the construction of meaningful global relationships.

Platforms such as LinkedIn, Twitter, and specific professional communities offer unprecedented opportunities to expand networks and cultivate strategic relationships. Studies indicate that 85% of positions are filled through networking, highlighting its fundamental importance.

Visibility, the fourth key element, has gained new contours with the algorithm of social networks and AI tools. Professionals who understand how to create relevant and engaging content are able to amplify their digital presence organically.

Consistency in content production, combined with a well-planned digital presence strategy, can turn professionals into references in their niches.

Professional empowerment, the fifth essential aspect, is directly related to autonomy and control over one's own career.

In a market where 40% of the workforce already participates in the gig economy, having a strong personal brand allows for greater independence in choosing projects and opportunities.

In addition, professionals with well-established personal brands are 27% more likely to be promoted and 31% more likely to receive significant salary increases.

Building a personal brand has also become fundamental for the development of professional resilience. In a volatile market, where linear careers are increasingly rare, a solid personal brand works as an anchor, allowing strategic pivots and adaptation to new opportunities without losing the professional essence.

Authenticity emerges as a differential element in the construction of the modern personal brand. In a world saturated with digital content, audiences increasingly value professionals who demonstrate genuineness in their interactions and communications.

This includes sharing not only successes but also learnings and challenges, creating deeper and more lasting connections.

The impact of personal branding extends beyond the individual professional sphere, influencing organizations and markets. Professionals with strong personal brands often become natural ambassadors for the companies where they work, contributing to employer branding and talent attraction.

Studies show that companies with employees active in professional networks are 58% more likely to attract high-quality talent.

To build an effective personal brand in the current context, it is necessary to:

- Develop strategic digital presence on relevant platforms.

- Create valuable content that demonstrates expertise and knowledge.

- Maintain consistency in communication and positioning.

- Invest in continuous development and professional updating.

- Cultivate authentic and meaningful relationships.

- Align personal values with professional actions.

- Monitor and adapt strategies based on metrics and feedback.

Keep in mind that building a personal brand has become a strategic imperative in the contemporary professional environment.

More than a personal marketing tool, it represents a fundamental investment in sustainable professional development and in building a resilient career aligned with personal and professional goals.

12.2   Strategic guide for building a powerful personal brand in the digital age.

Building an effective personal brand in the digital age requires a strategic, multifaceted approach that goes beyond simply an online presence.

The first fundamental pillar is deep self-knowledge. This process goes beyond simply identifying technical skills.

With the help of behavioral analysis tools and AI-based personality tests, professionals can map not only their values and talents, but also identify patterns of behavior and areas of excellence that have set them apart in the market.

Recent studies show that professionals with a high level of self-knowledge are 36% more likely to reach leadership positions.

Visual identity, the second crucial element, has gained new dimensions with emerging technologies. It's not just about creating a logo, but about developing a coherent visual presence across platforms.

AI-powered design tools allow you to create professional visual identities that automatically adapt to different platforms and formats.

Color palette choice should consider color psychology and current digital trends, with 85% of consumers citing color as a primary factor in a brand's perception.

The development of a powerful personal narrative has become essential in the age of digital storytelling. The professional story should be structured following transmedia storytelling principles, allowing different aspects to be highlighted on different platforms.

Research indicates that well-constructed stories are 22 times more memorable than isolated facts. The narrative should include not only achievements, but also learnings from failures, creating a more authentic connection with the audience.

Building an online presence has evolved significantly.

LinkedIn remains the primary professional platform, but the current strategy calls for a coordinated multiplatform presence. Data shows that 92% of recruiters use social media in the hiring process.

The modern professional profile should include:

- LinkedIn optimized with strategic keywords.

- Interactive and responsive digital portfolio.

- Active presence in relevant professional communities.

- Content in different formats (text, audio, video).

- Personalized newsletter for qualified networking.

- Participation in virtual events and industry webinars.

Authenticity has become a crucial competitive differentiator. With the rise in distrust of digital content, demonstrating genuine authenticity has become critical.

This includes:

- Transparent sharing of professional experiences.

- Clear positioning on relevant issues in the sector.

- Demonstration of controlled vulnerability.

- Genuine engagement with the professional community.

- Consistency between message and actions.

Consistency in communication takes on new importance with social media algorithms prioritizing regular and engaging content.

A strategic content plan should include:

- Multiplatform editorial calendar.

- Mix of proprietary and curated content.

- Data-driven engagement metrics and adjustments.

- Regular interaction with followers and network.

- Constant updating of knowledge and trends.

New trends in personal branding include:

1. Personal Branding Audio:

- Personal podcasts.

- Participation in clubhouses and audio spaces

- Narratives in audio format.

2. Video Branding:

- Strategic lives.

- Short videos for social networks.

- Specialized webinars.

3. Data and Analytics:

- Monitoring of engagement metrics.

- Content performance analysis.

- Adjustments based on data insights.

4. Automation and AI:

- Content scheduling tools.

- Predictive trend analysis.

- Personalization of communication.

5. Digital Networking:

- Participation in online communities.

- Strategic collaborations.

- Virtual mentoring.

To maintain a relevant personal brand, it is essential to:

- Monitor industry trends and adapt strategies.

- Invest in continuous skill development.

- Maintain active professional relationships.

- Evaluate and adjust positioning regularly.

- Seek constant feedback from the professional network.

Success in building a modern personal brand depends on the ability to balance authenticity with strategy, consistency with innovation, and digital presence with genuine connections.

In a world where 76% of professional opportunities come through networking, a well-built personal brand becomes a key strategic asset for career development.

Extra tips:

- ✓ Attend events: Connect with other professionals at events in your field.

- ✓ Seek out mentors: Find a mentor who can guide you in your career.

- ✓ Ask for feedback: Ask for feedback from people you trust to improve your personal brand.

- ✓ Adapt your brand: Your personal brand should evolve over time, so be open to change.

Building a personal brand is an ongoing process. With dedication and consistency, you will be able to stand out in the job market and achieve your professional goals.

13 AI Market Overview: Growth Sectors.

The Artificial Intelligence (AI) market is constantly expanding, driven by technological advancements and the growing demand from businesses for innovative solutions.

Several sectors are being transformed by AI, creating a scenario of great opportunities for qualified professionals.

Featured sectors:

- Technology: development of software, hardware, and AI platforms.

- Health: diagnosis of diseases, development of medicines, personalization of treatments.

- Finance: fraud detection, risk analysis, investment recommendation.

- Marketing: personalization of campaigns, analysis of customer data, content creation.

- Industrial automation: process optimization, predictive maintenance, robotics.

- Transportation: autonomous vehicles, route optimization, fleet management.

13.1   Top job titles and areas of expertise for AI specialists.

The AI market offers a wide range of career opportunities for professionals with different skills and interests.

Some of the key positions and areas of expertise include:

- Data scientist. Collects, cleanses, and analyzes large volumes of data to extract insights and build AI models.

- Machine learning engineer. Develops and implements machine learning algorithms to solve specific problems.

- AI Engineer. It develops and implements AI solutions in different business areas.

- Computer vision specialist. He works with images and videos to develop object recognition systems, face detection, etc.

- Specialist in natural language processing (NLP). He works with text and language to develop chatbots, machine translation systems, etc.

- AI Solutions Architect. Develops the architecture of complex AI systems.

- AI ethicist. It evaluates the ethical implications of the development and use of AI systems.

13.2   How to highlight your IT expertise and position yourself in the AI market.

To stand out in the AI market, it is essential to combine your IT knowledge with specific skills in the area. Some tips to position yourself:

- Develop technical skills. Mastering programming languages like Python, R, and frameworks like TensorFlow and PyTorch is essential.

- Deepen knowledge in statistics and mathematics. A solid foundation in statistics and mathematics is critical to understanding machine learning algorithms.

- Work on personal projects. Develop hands-on projects to demonstrate your skills and build a portfolio.

- Participate in online communities. Interact with other professionals in the field, participate in forums and discussion groups.

- Certifications. Get certifications on platforms like Coursera, edX, and Udemy to validate your knowledge.

- Networking. Build a solid network of contacts to stay up-to-date on the latest trends and job opportunities.

- Personal marketing. Create an attractive professional profile on social media and job search platforms.

Additional tips:

- ✓ Specialize in one area. By specializing in a specific area of AI, you become more attractive to companies.

- ✓ Stay up to date. The field of AI is constantly evolving, so it's important to keep up with the latest news and trends.

- ✓ Adapt. Be willing to learn new technologies and adapt to market changes.

By following these tips, you will be well-prepared to build a successful career in the field of Artificial Intelligence.

14 How to grow in your new career: from expert to leader.

Transitioning from an AI expert to a leadership position requires more than just technical expertise. It is necessary to develop management, communication and strategic vision skills. For this evolution, consider the following steps:

- Develop your leadership skills: look for courses and training in leadership, team management, and conflict resolution.

- Broaden your strategic vision: Understand the business as a whole and how AI can contribute to the company's growth.

- Build relationships: Cultivate relationships with colleagues, superiors, and stakeholders.

- Effective communication: Be able to communicate complex ideas clearly and concisely to different audiences.

- Mentoring: look for an experienced mentor who can guide you on this journey.

14.1   Long-term strategies to stay relevant in the AI market.

The Artificial Intelligence market is experiencing an unprecedented transformation, driven primarily by the emergence of increasingly sophisticated models such as ChatGPT, Claude, and Gemini.

To stay competitive in this dynamic landscape, it has become essential to adopt a multi-faceted approach to professional development.

Continuous learning emerges as a fundamental pillar, requiring not only keeping up with the latest trends and technologies, but also active participation in specialized courses, international conferences, and practical workshops focused on areas such as deep learning, natural language processing, and computer vision.

Strategic networking has gained even more relevance, especially with the expansion of remote work and virtual developer communities.

Building a solid network of contacts, whether through platforms such as LinkedIn, GitHub or Discord, has proven crucial for the exchange of experiences and collaborative learning.

The development of personal projects also stands out as a competitive advantage, allowing practical experimentation with new technologies such as transformers, neural networks, and optimization algorithms.

The dissemination of knowledge through technical publications, whether in specialized blogs, scientific articles or presentations at industry events, has proven to be an effective strategy to build authority in the area.

Additionally, specializing in specific AI niches, such as AI ethics, generative AI, or AI applied to specific industries such as healthcare or finance, has proven to be a promising path to stand out in the market.

This set of practices, when implemented consistently, not only contributes to individual professional growth but also to the collective advancement of the field of Artificial Intelligence.

14.2   The importance of continuous learning.

Continuous learning is essential for any professional, especially for those who work in the area of Artificial Intelligence (AI).

The rapid evolution of AI, machine learning, and deep learning technologies requires experts to always be up-to-date with the latest innovations, techniques, and tools.

It's not just about learning new programming languages or mastering new frameworks, but about understanding emerging trends and being able to anticipate market needs.

One of the main benefits of continuous learning is adaptability. The technology sector is known for its speed of transformation, and within AI, this is even more evident. New algorithms, advances in neural networks, and changes in market demands can occur at an accelerated pace.

A professional who is constantly learning is able to quickly adjust to these changes, ensuring that their skills are always aligned with the latest in the world. This also makes it easier to transition into new areas, such as Natural Language Processing (NLP), Computer Vision, or AI applied to robotics.

Another benefit is innovation. Continuous learning not only allows you to keep up with technical progress, but also stimulates the development of new solutions and ideas.

Professionals who invest in their own development have a greater ability to think creatively and apply the knowledge acquired to solve complex problems or find new business opportunities.

In a landscape where AI is being used to transform industries such as healthcare, finance, and logistics, being one of the first to master new tools and algorithms can make a big difference.

Additionally, continuous learning ensures that you remain competitive in the job market. As AI becomes more widespread, the number of professionals seeking positions in this field grows.

Staying ahead of the competition requires a dedication to learning that goes beyond the basics, seeking to master advanced topics such as deep neural networks, reinforcement learning, and the integration of AI with big data.

Professionals who are up to date are more likely to occupy prominent positions, lead innovative projects, and become references in their companies or sectors.

Finally, continuous learning contributes significantly to job satisfaction. The field of AI is full of intellectual challenges and offers numerous opportunities for growth.

By committing to constant development, the professional has the opportunity to solve complex problems, participate in innovative projects and, consequently, feel more fulfilled in their career.

Each new skill acquired not only broadens your technical repertoire, but also opens doors to new opportunities, whether in tech startups, large corporations, or academia.

In a highly competitive global landscape, continuous learning stands out as a strategic advantage. It not only ensures longevity and professional relevance, but also enables AI professionals to shape the future of technology by developing solutions that profoundly impact society and business.

Therefore, investing in yourself and your learning is an indispensable strategy for those who want to not only survive, but thrive in the age of Artificial Intelligence.

Ways to learn continuously:

- Online courses: Platforms like Coursera, edX, and Udemy offer a variety of courses in AI.

- Books and articles: Read books and articles about the latest trends in the field.

- Workshops and conferences: Attend events to connect with other professionals and learn about what's new in the market.

- Personal projects: develop projects to apply your knowledge in practice.

- Mentoring: Seek an experienced mentor to guide you on your journey.

15 Strategic Roadmap for the Career Transition from IT to Artificial Intelligence: Key Topics and Steps.

Transitioning from a traditional career in information technology (IT) to artificial intelligence (AI) requires a change in mindset, an adaptation of skills, and a continuous learning effort.

For IT professionals looking to navigate this new landscape, the process may seem challenging, but with the proper guidance and a well-defined strategy, the transition can be not only feasible but extremely rewarding.

This guide presents a detailed roadmap for this transformation, highlighting key areas of study, recommended resources, and realistic learning timelines for each step.

1. Fundamentals in Mathematics and Statistics: The Basis for AI

Before entering the universe of artificial intelligence, it is essential that the IT professional solidifies his foundation in mathematics and statistics. These concepts form the foundation upon which AI models are built.

Mastering topics such as linear algebra, calculus, and probability allows the professional to deeply understand machine learning and deep learning algorithms.

Recommendation:

Dedicate 3-6 months to reviewing or learning these concepts, depending on your previous level of familiarity.

Suggested Features:

Coursera offers both free and paid courses that cover everything from fundamentals to advanced topics.

Khan Academy is an excellent resource for learning math in an accessible and structured way.

MIT OpenCourseWare offers math and statistics courses from one of the world's most renowned universities, allowing you to learn at your own pace.

2. Relevant Programming Languages: The Heart of AI

Fluency in programming languages such as Python and R is crucial for any professional who wants to work with artificial intelligence. Python, with its specific libraries like TensorFlow, PyTorch, and scikit-learn, has become the preferred language among data scientists and AI engineers for its versatility and ease of use.

Estimated Time:

2-4 months to acquire basic proficiency in Python and R.

6-12 months to reach an advanced level.

3. Machine Learning: The Core of AI

Machine learning is the fundamental pillar on which many AI solutions are developed.

Starting with supervised algorithms, such as linear regression and decision trees, and unsupervised algorithms, such as clustering, is one way to establish a solid foundation.

As you move forward, you should focus on more complex techniques, such as deep learning and neural networks, which are at the forefront of modern AI.

Recommended Courses:

Machine Learning, by Andrew Ng, offered on Coursera, is widely recognized as an excellent introduction to the topic.

The Fast.ai course offers a practical and accelerated approach for those who already have a foundation and want to apply AI efficiently.

Duration:

3-6 months to master the fundamentals of machine learning.

6-12 months for proficiency in deep learning and neural networks.

4. Data Analysis and Visualization Skills: Turning Data into Decisions

Data analysis and visualization are crucial steps in the lifecycle of AI projects. Tools such as Tableau and Power BI allow professionals to interpret and communicate insights extracted from large volumes of data in a visual and intuitive way.

These competencies are particularly important in business scenarios where decisions need to be data-driven.

Estimated Time:

2-3 months to gain proficiency in key data visualization tools and practices with real datasets.

5. Understanding the Business and Ethical Context of AI

As AI solutions become more widespread across different industries, it is vital for professionals to understand the business context in which these technologies are implemented.

AI use cases in areas such as healthcare, finance, and logistics are becoming commonplace, but it is also crucial to consider the ethical impact of these applications, especially when it comes to data privacy and fairness in algorithms.

Recommended Reading:

AI Ethics, by Mark Coeckelbergh, offers a critical look at the ethical challenges that come with the large-scale adoption of AI.

Duration:

While understanding this context is an ongoing process, dedicate at least 1-2 months for an initial in-depth study.

6. Hands-on Experience: The Value of Learning by Doing

Theoretical knowledge is not enough; it is essential to gain hands-on experience in AI. Working on personal projects, participating in competitions on platforms like Kaggle, and contributing to open-source projects are all effective ways to put what you've learned into practice.

Estimated Time:

3-6 months to build an initial portfolio of hands-on AI projects.

7. Networking: The Support Network for Continued Growth

Building a solid network of contacts can accelerate career transition by providing access to learning, collaboration, and employment opportunities. Attending conferences, webinars, and online discussion groups such as Reddit and Stack Overflow are all effective strategies for connecting with the AI community.

Frequency:

Weekly activity, with participation in events quarterly.

8. Relevant Certifications: Validating Your Expertise

Obtaining internationally recognized certifications in AI can provide a competitive advantage in the job market.

Certifications such as the TensorFlow Developer Certificate or the AWS Machine Learning Specialty validate the skills and knowledge of the professional, helping them to excel in the field.

Estimated Time:

1-3 months for certification.

9. Staying Updated: Keeping Up with Trends in AI

AI is an ever-evolving field. To remain competitive, the professional must dedicate himself to continuous learning. Subscribing to newsletters, such as Import AI, reading academic articles regularly, and participating in hackathons are all effective ways to keep up with news and trends.

Frequency:

Dedicate a few hours a week to reading and updating.

1.5 Transition Time Forecast: The Time Required According to Experience Level

The duration of the transition process varies according to the professional's level of experience. An IT student can take up to 2 years to make the complete transition, while a senior professional with extensive experience can achieve this transformation in less than a year.

IT student: 1-2 years.

Professional Trainee: 1-1.5 years.

Full Professional: 9-18 months.

Senior Professional: 6-12 months.

1.6 Analysis by IT Professional Profile: Where to Focus

Professionals from different areas of IT have unique advantages and challenges in the transition to AI.

For example, DBAs have a strong understanding of data structures, but they may encounter difficulties when dealing with unstructured data models.

Developers, on the other hand, have a solid foundation in programming, but they need to adapt to the new paradigms of AI.

Regardless of the profile, the key to success is continuous learning and a willingness to adopt new technologies, applying existing IT knowledge in new contexts driven by artificial intelligence.

The journey of an AI professional is marked by constant learning and evolution. By developing your technical and leadership skills, building a solid network of contacts, and investing in your continuous learning, you will be prepared to face the challenges of the market and achieve success in your career.

16 References

ABBYY. Intelligent Automation for Document Processing. ABBYY Research, 2019.

AGGARWAL, Charu C. Neural Networks and Deep Learning: A Textbook. Cham: Springer, 2018.

ALPAYDIN, Ethem. Introduction to Machine Learning. 4. ed. Cambridge: MIT Press, 2020.

BISHOP, Christopher M. Pattern Recognition and Machine Learning. New York: Springer, 2006.

BOSTROM, N. Superintelligence: Paths, Dangers, Strategies. Oxford University Press, 2014.

CHARLTON, Paul; YAKUBOVIC, Boris. Practical Artificial Intelligence: Machine Learning, Bots, and Agent Solutions Using C#. Berkeley: Apress, 2020.

CHOLETTE, François. Deep Learning with Python. 2. ed. Shelter Island: Manning Publications, 2021.

COECKELBERGH, Mark. AI Ethics. MIT Press, 2020.

COHEN, J.E. Configuring the Networked Self: Law, Code, and the Play of Everyday Practice. Yale University Press, 2012.

DOMINGOS, Pedro. The Master Algorithm: How the Quest for the Ultimate Learning Machine Will Remake Our World. New York: Basic Books, 2015.

GÉRON, Aurélien. Hands-On Machine Learning with Scikit-Learn, Keras, and TensorFlow: Concepts, Tools, and Techniques to Build Intelligent Systems. 2. ed. Sebastopol: O'Reilly Media, 2019.

GITHUB. GitHub Copilot: Your AI Pair Programmer. GitHub Documentation, 2021.

GOODFELLOW, Ian; BENGIO, Yoshua; COURVILLE, Aaron. Deep Learning. Cambridge: MIT Press, 2016.

HASTIE, Trevor; TIBSHIRANI, Robert; FRIEDMAN, Jerome. The Elements of Statistical Learning: Data Mining, Inference, and Prediction. 2nd ed. New York: Springer, 2009.

JAMES, Gareth; WITTEN, Daniela; HASTIE, Trevor; TIBSHIRANI, Robert. An Introduction to Statistical Learning: With Applications in R. New York: Springer, 2013.

JORDAN, Michael I.; MITCHELL, Tom M. Machine Learning: Trends, Perspectives, and Prospects. Science, v. 349, n. 6245, p. 255–260, 2015.

KOLTER, J. Zico. Machine Learning for Healthcare. Cambridge: MIT Press, 2021.

MCKINSEY & COMPANY. The Future of Work in Technology. McKinsey Global Institute, 2020.

MITCHELL, Tom M. Machine Learning. 1st ed. New York: McGraw-Hill, 1997.

MURPHY, Kevin P. Machine Learning: A Probabilistic Perspective. Cambridge: MIT Press, 2012.

NG, Andrew. Machine Learning Yearning. Palo Alto: deeplearning.ai, 2019.

NG, Andrew. Machine Learning. Coursera, 2018.

NIELSEN, Michael A. Neural Networks and Deep Learning: A Visual Introduction to Deep Learning. San Francisco: Determination Press, 2015.

ORACLE. Oracle Autonomous Database: Overview. Oracle Corporation, 2018.

RAJ, Abhishek; BHATNAGAR, Ankit; KUMAR, Himanshu. Machine Learning Using Python: Easy and Practical Methods for Beginners. New York: Packt Publishing, 2019.

RUSSELL, S.; NORVIG, P. Artificial Intelligence: A Modern Approach. 4. ed. Pearson, 2020.

SCHAPIRE, Robert; FREUND, Yoav. Boosting: Foundations and Algorithms. Cambridge: MIT Press, 2014.

SEPTIMUS, O. Artificial Intelligence and the Future of Project Management. Cambridge University Press, 2022.

17 Conclusion.

Throughout this book, we explore the transition path from an IT professional to an artificial intelligence specialist, offering a detailed look at the changes and opportunities that AI provides.

We discussed how the evolution of technology is transforming traditional IT functions such as programming, database management, and technical support, and saw how these areas are benefiting from automation and autonomous intelligence.

The uniqueness of AI lies not only in its ability to replace repetitive functions, but also in creating new fields of activity for professionals who are willing to learn and innovate.

We examine the similarities and differences between the fields of IT and AI, and how the merging of these fields is shaping the future of technology.

The book offered an essential learning path for those who want to specialize in machine learning, deep learning, neural networks, and natural language processing (NLP), as well as highlighting the technical and theoretical skills needed to stand out in the market.

The technical and emotional challenges of transition were realistically addressed, from the learning curve to overcoming internal and external resistance to change.

We also show the importance of a strategic portfolio, demonstrating how your AI projects can be instrumental in highlighting your competencies in the competitive job market.

Finally, this book emphasized the importance of adopting a continuous growth mindset, allowing you to stay relevant in a field as dynamic and challenging as artificial intelligence.

However, this is just one step in an essential journey in the field of artificial intelligence. This volume is part of a larger collection, "Artificial Intelligence: The Power of Data," which explores, in depth, different aspects of AI and data science.

The other volumes address equally crucial topics, such as the integration of AI systems, predictive analytics, and the use of advanced algorithms for decision-making.

By purchasing and reading the other books in the collection, you will have a holistic and deep view that will allow you not only to optimize data governance, but also to enhance the impact of artificial intelligence on your operations. Take advantage of this opportunity to learn, apply, and lead in the age of AI!

"Every great dream begins with a dreamer. Always remember that you have within you the strength, patience, and passion to reach for the stars to change the world."

Harriet Tubman[1]

---

[1] Harriet Tubman (née Araminta Ross; c. 1820 or 1821 – March 10, 1913) was an American abolitionist and political activist. Born into slavery, Tubman escaped and subsequently went on about thirteen missions to rescue approximately seventy enslaved people, including family and friends, using the network of anti-slavery activists and safe houses known as the Underground Railroad. During the American Civil War, she served as a spy for the Union army. After the war, Tubman was an activist in the women's suffrage movement.

18 Artificial Intelligence Collection: the power of data.

The collection, written by Prof. Marcão, offers a deep immersion in the universe of Artificial Intelligence (AI), a technology that is transforming the world irreversibly. In a series of carefully crafted books, the author explores complex concepts in an accessible way, providing the reader with a broad understanding of AI and its impact on modern societies.

The central goal of the collection is to empower the reader to understand what is behind the technology that drives today's world, from its practical applications in everyday life to the ethical and philosophical debates that emerge as AI advances.

Each volume focuses on specific and fundamental aspects of the theme, with explanations based on both academic research and the author's practical experience, making the work indispensable for anyone who wants to navigate this field essential to the future.

18.1   Why study the ARTIFICIAL INTELLIGENCE AND THE POWER OF DATA collection?

We are experiencing an unprecedented technological revolution, where AI plays a central role in sectors such as medicine, entertainment, finance, education, and government.

With a writing that combines clarity and depth, Prof. Marcão's collection makes the topic accessible to both laymen and specialists.

In addition to exploring facts, the work offers reflections on the social, cultural, and ethical impact of AI, encouraging the reader to rethink their relationship with technology.

18.2   Who is the collection suitable for?

The collection "ARTIFICIAL INTELLIGENCE AND THE POWER OF DATA" is aimed at a wide range of readers. Tech professionals will find deep technical insights, while students and the curious will have access to clear and accessible explanations.

Managers, business leaders, and policymakers will also benefit from AI's strategic understanding, which is essential for making informed decisions.

Prof. Marcão offers a complete approach, addressing both technical aspects and the strategic implications of AI in the current scenario.

18.3   The intellectual and practical value of the collection.

More than a series of technical books, this collection is a tool for intellectual transformation. Prof. Marcão invites the reader to reflect on the future of humanity in a world where machines and algorithms are increasingly present in our lives.

19 The books of the Collection.

19.1   Data, information and knowledge.

This book essentially explores the theoretical and practical foundations of Artificial Intelligence, from data collection to its transformation into intelligence.

Focusing on machine learning, AI training, and neural networks, the work is indispensable for professionals and scholars seeking to understand the challenges and opportunities of AI.

19.2   Data into gold: how to turn information into wisdom in the age of AI.

This book looks at the evolution of artificial intelligence from raw data to building artificial wisdom, combining neural networks, deep learning, and knowledge modeling.

With practical examples in healthcare, finance, and education, and addressing ethical and technical challenges, it is ideal for anyone seeking to understand the transformative impact of AI.

19.3   Challenges and limitations of data in AI.

The book offers an in-depth analysis of the role of data in the development of AI exploring topics such as quality, bias, privacy, security, and scalability.

With practical case studies in healthcare, finance, and public safety, it is an essential guide for professionals and researchers seeking to understand how data shapes the future of artificial intelligence.

19.4 Historics are not a thing of the past.

This book explores how data management, especially historical data, is critical to the success of AI projects. It addresses the relevance of ISO standards to ensure quality and safety, in addition to analyzing trends and innovations in data processing.

With a practical approach, it is an indispensable resource for professionals focused on efficient data management in the age of AI.

19.5 Controlled vocabulary.

This comprehensive guide looks at the advantages and challenges of implementing controlled vocabularies in the context of AI and information science.

With a detailed approach, it covers everything from the naming of data elements to the interactions between semantics and cognition. Essential for professionals and researchers looking to optimize data management and the development of AI systems.

19.6 Data Management for AI.

The book presents advanced strategies for transforming raw data into powerful insights, with a focus on meticulous curation and efficient management.

In addition to technical solutions, it addresses ethical and legal issues, empowering the reader to face the complex challenges of information.

Whether you're a manager, data scientist, or AI enthusiast, and for professionals looking to master data management in the digital age.

19.7   Information architecture.

Essential guide for professionals who want to master data management in the digital age, combining theory and practice to create efficient and scalable AI systems.

With insights into modeling, ethical and legal challenges, it is ideal for data scientists, AI engineers, and IT managers looking to turn data into actionable intelligence and gain competitive advantage.

19.8   Fundamentals.

Essential work for those who want to master the key concepts of AI, with an accessible approach and practical examples.

The book explores innovations such as Machine Learning and Natural Language Processing, as well as ethical and legal challenges, and offers a clear view of the impact of AI on various industries, ideal for professionals and technology enthusiasts.

19.9   Large language models – LLMs.

Essential guide to understanding the language model revolution (LLMs) in AI.

The book explores the evolution of GPTs and the latest innovations in human-computer interaction, offering practical insights into their impact on industries such as healthcare, education, and finance. Indispensable for professionals, researchers, and AI enthusiasts.

19.10 Machine learning.

This book is essential for professionals and enthusiasts who want to master revolutionary areas of AI. It offers a comprehensive overview of supervised and unsupervised algorithms, deep neural networks, and federated learning.

With discussions on the ethics and explainability of models, it prepares the reader for the challenges and opportunities of AI in sectors such as healthcare, finance, and public safety.

19.11 Synthetic minds.

A must-read for anyone looking to explore the future of generative AIs, this book reveals how these "synthetic minds" are redefining creativity, work, and human interactions.

Aimed at technology professionals, content creators, and the curious, it offers an in-depth analysis of the challenges and opportunities of these technologies, reflecting on their impact on society.

19.12 The issue of copyright.

This book is a thought-provoking invitation to explore the future of creativity in a world where humans and machines collaborate, addressing questions about authorship, originality, and intellectual property in the age of generative AIs.

Ideal for professionals, creators and innovation enthusiasts, it offers deep reflections and challenges you to rethink the balance between technology and creators' rights.

19.13   Questions and Answers from Basics to Complex – Volumes 1 to 4.

The questions, organized into 4 volumes, are essential practical guides to master the main concepts of AI.

The 1121 questions address topics such as Machine Learning, Natural Language Processing and Computer Vision, offering clear and concise answers.

Ideal for professionals, students, and enthusiasts, the book combines didactic explanations with insights into ethics, data privacy, and the challenges of AI helping to transform your knowledge and explore the potential of this revolutionary technology.

Part 1 includes:

- Information, data and geoprocessing.
- Evolution of artificial intelligence.
- AI milestones.
- Basic concepts and definitions.

Part 2 includes:

- Complex concepts.
- Machine learning.
- Natural language processing.
- Computer vision and robotics.
- Decision algorithms.

Part 3 includes:

- Data privacy.
- Automation of work.
- Large-scale language models - LLMs.

Part 4 includes:

- The role of data in the age of artificial intelligence.
- Fundamentals of artificial intelligence.
- Government, politics and the fight against corruption.
- Mental health.

19.14   Glossary.

With more than a thousand concepts selected from the context of artificial intelligence clearly explained, the book addresses topics such as Machine Learning, Natural Language Processing, Computer Vision and AI Ethics.

Ideal for professionals and the curious, the work offers a comprehensive overview of the impact of AI on society.

- Part 1 contemplates concepts starting with the letters A to D.
- Part 2 contemplates concepts initiated by the letters E to M.
- Part 3 contemplates concepts starting with the letters N to Z.

19.15   Prompt engineering: volumes 1 to 6.

The collection covers all the fundamental themes of prompt engineering, providing a complete professional development.

With a rich variety of prompts for areas such as leadership, digital marketing, and information technology, it offers practical examples to improve clarity, decision-making, and gain valuable insights.

Ideal for professionals, entrepreneurs, and students, this guide reveals how to use the power of prompts to turn ideas into concrete actions and drive impressive results.

The volumes cover the following subjects:

- Volume 1: deals with the fundamentals. structuring concepts and history of prompt engineering.

- Volume 2: Covers Tools and Technologies, State and Context Management, and Ethics and Security.
- Volume 3: Looks at language models, tokenization, and training methods.
- Volume 4: will teach you the techniques to ask correct questions.
- Volume 5: presents and analyzes case studies and errors.
- Volume 6: is your essential guide with the best prompts.

With an extensive collection of practical prompts, the book offers everything from tips for effective communication and decision-making to suggestions for personal development, career, marketing, and information technology.

19.16 Guide to Being a Prompt Engineer – Volumes 1 and 2.

The collection explores the advanced fundamentals and skills required to be a successful prompt engineer, highlighting the benefits, risks, and the critical role this role plays in the development of artificial intelligence.

Volume 1 covers crafting effective prompts, and volume 2 is your guide to understanding and applying the fundamentals of Prompt Engineering.

For those looking to optimize their interactions with AI, the book is a must-have for technology professionals.

19.17   Data governance.

Find out how to implement effective data governance with this comprehensive collection. Offering practical guidance, the books range from data architecture management to protection and quality, providing a complete view for transforming data into strategic assets.

Volume 1 addresses practices and regulations. Volume 2 explores in depth the processes, techniques, and best practices for conducting effective audits on data models. Volume 3 is your definitive guide to deploying data governance with AI.

Ideal for IT specialists, managers, and enthusiasts, it is the definitive resource to ensure compliance, security, and efficiency in data management.

19.18   Algorithm Governance.

This book analyzes the impact of algorithms on society, exploring everything from their foundations to ethical and regulatory issues.

It addresses transparency, accountability, and bias, with practical solutions for auditing and monitoring algorithms in sectors such as finance, health, and education.

Ideal for professionals and managers, it offers an ethical and sustainable view of digital governance.

19.19   From IT to AI: the transition guide.

For Information Technology professionals, the transition to AI represents an opportunity to enhance their skills and contribute to the development of innovative solutions that drive the future.

In this book, we explore the reasons for making this transition, the essential skills, a practical roadmap, and the prospects for the future of the IT job market.

Ideal for IT professionals who want to make a career transition to being an artificial intelligence professional.

19.20   Intelligent leadership with AI - transform your team and drive results

This book reveals how artificial intelligence can revolutionize team management and maximize organizational performance.

By combining traditional leadership techniques with AI-powered insights, you'll learn how to optimize processes, make more strategic decisions, and create more efficient and engaged teams.

Aimed at managers, business leaders, consultants, and professionals who want to improve their leadership skills in an increasingly digital world, this book offers practical and accessible strategies for implementing AI in the day-to-day of team management. If you're looking to take your team to the next level, this is the essential guide.

19.21   Impacts and transformations.

The collection covers everything from the technical and ethical challenges of detecting AI-generated text, to the influence of algorithms on our digital lives and the transformation of content creation.

The collection also discusses the future of humanity in light of the technological singularity and the dangers of disinformation in the digital age, where artificial intelligence can be used to manipulate public opinion.

1. Volume 1: Challenges and Solutions in the Detection of AI-generated texts.
2. Volume 2: The Age of Filter Bubbles.
3. Volume 3: Content Creation.
4. Volume 4: The singularity is near.
5. Volume 5: Real Stupidity Versus Artificial Intelligence
6. Volume 6: The Age of Stupidity: A Cult of Stupidity.
7. Volume 7: Autonomy on the move: the smart vehicle revolution.
8. Volume 8: Poiesis and creativity with AI.

Ideal for IT professionals, politicians, academics, urban planners and technology enthusiasts, the collection reveals the social, economic and ethical impacts of this transformation, addressing the reconfiguration of society, cities and the labor market.

"In the information age, knowledge is power, but true wisdom lies in the ability to discern and wisely utilize the vastness of available data."

Brian Herbert[2]

---

[2] American author known for his works in the field of science fiction, especially for having co-written several works set in the universe created by his father, Frank Herbert, in the "Dune" book series.

20 Meet the author. A researcher always in search of knowledge.

I'm Marcus Pinto, known as Prof. Marcão, a specialist in information technology, information architecture and artificial intelligence. With a solid career, I bring you this collection of books, the result of extensive research and study, with the aim of making technical knowledge accessible and applicable.

My experience as a consultant, educator and writer and as an information architecture analyst for more than 40 years allows me to work in strategic areas, offering innovative solutions that meet the growing needs of the technological market.

Over decades, I have developed expertise in data, information, and artificial intelligence, crucial areas for the creation of robust systems that process the immensity of data generated in the contemporary world.

With works available on Amazon, I offer content that addresses topics such as Data Governance, Big Data and Artificial Intelligence, always focused on practical application and strategic vision.

Author of more than 150 books, he studies the impact of artificial intelligence in various fields, from its technical foundations to the ethical implications of its use.

In my lectures and mentorships, I share not only the relevance of AI, but also the challenges and precautions necessary for an ethical and responsible adoption of these technologies.

Technological evolution is inevitable, and my books offer the way for those who wish to not only understand, but master the future. With a focus on education and human development, I invite you to explore this transformative journey through my works.

21 How to contact prof. Marcão.

21.1   For lectures, training and business mentoring.

marcao.tecno@gmail.com

Consulting   and   Training   Company: https://mvpconsult.com.br

21.2   Prof. Marcão on Linkedin.

https://bit.ly/linkedin_profmarcao